Collins *gem*

Dictators

GW00492619

Sean Callery

HarperCollins Publishers
Westerhill Road, Bishopriggs, Glasgow, G64 2QT

www.collins.co.uk

First published 2007
Text © Sean Callery, 2007
10 09 08 07
10 9 8 7 6 5 4 3 2 1

A catalogue record for this book is available from the British
Library

Managing editor: Louise Stanley
Designer: Roy Platten
Proofreading: Donald Sommerville

ISBN-13: 978-0-00-724221-4
ISBN-10: 0-00-724221-2

Printed and bound by Printing Express Ltd, Hong Kong

CONTENTS

INTRODUCTION

History may be written by the victors, but it is made by bullies – the tyrants, despots and warlords who take it upon themselves to boss everybody else about and who are sufficiently lacking in morality to kill off those who pose a threat.

What is a dictator?

A dictator is someone who appoints themselves to take over a government – often using violence – and who maintains absolute power through the state's institutions, such as the army, the economy and the law system (which they generally corrupt).

This particular definition, however, doesn't apply to the early dictators. The word dictator is Latin and was used in the Roman Republic when it was decided that, under certain circumstances, the two consuls normally in power should be replaced by a 'master of the people' who would be put in absolute control for a short time, such as during a war or disaster. His decisions were final, and he could not be held accountable for them by law. The first leader to try to hold onto power for life was Julius Caesar. His great nephew Augustus carried on the family tradition and features in this book (page 20).

The epithet of dictator, though, has been applied to many despots who wielded absolute power well before the days of the Romans, such as Pheidon of Argos (page 14) – arguably the first dictator in all but name. Many of them at the time (and since) would not have regarded themselves as tyrants, but as strong rulers bringing unity to their people. Indeed, some dictators are viewed by their subjects as having improved the lot of their country, providing the origin for the term 'benevolent despotism', embodied by leaders such as Peter the Great and Hastings Kamuzu Banda.

However, dictator is widely applied to describe ruthlessly violent absolute rulers who turn a country into a personal fiefdom and, for glory and personal gain, either rob it or turn it into their private army, or both.

Why does it happen?

Dictators often gain power during times of disorder. In war, famine, economic breakdown or social turmoil, people are ready for change if they believe it will bring stability. For example, Hitler came to power when Germany had all but broken down under the perceived injustice of the post-World War One Versailles Treaty. He gained widespread support after he rose to power by blaming Germany's ills on the Jews, liberals and Communists, whom he believed were the 'enemies within'. He also promised economic stability and to restore Germany to her pre-war state. In the right circumstances, it is possible for a dictator to achieve power via the democratic process by being (usually briefly) regarded as a saviour. Given a divided opposition, you don't need to achieve a massive vote to get into office.

What sort of person becomes a dictator?
It helps to be male: there have been very few female dictators (there is only one in this book), partly because throughout history very few women have been allowed to become rulers, and perhaps because female nature doesn't necessarily fit with the typical profile of a despot. Some common characteristics and experiences of dictators are:

- A violent or absent father (see Hitler, Franco, Chiang Kai-shek);

- Being sufficiently rebellious or immoral to flout the law (both Timur and Saddam Hussein stole in their younger years);

- A reasonable education;

- Service in the army – good for learning how to give orders and for building a power base;

- Immorality – many dictators were notorious womanisers;

- Charisma – Peron, for example, was a great public speaker with a gift for the common touch;

■ Rampant egotism – many dictators set about creating their own personality cult (see Kim Il-sung, Josef Stalin and Saparmurat Niyazov);

■ Greed – many dictators have amassed huge fortunes, or have been obsessive collectors (Trujillo had a vast number of neckties, Mao a huge store of pornography, and Imelda Marcos famously had more stilettos than she could wear in a lifetime).

TOP TEN TIPS FOR TYRANTS

Join the army

Dictators frequently have military backgrounds. Obviously, having access to weapons and a force able to use them is crucial if you intend to threaten or enact violence. Another reason is that the army takes up much of the budget of a small country, so senior members have a political interest in the government because it maintains their own positions. If you have been part of the military, it is more likely to stay loyal to you, too. Once you gain power, put yourself in charge of the military or they will plot against you.

Show no mercy

Early on, butcher as many as you wish, and spread the word; fear is a powerful way of suppressing dissent. The slightest glimmer of mercy is seen as weakness.

If you must have elections, rig them

Even if you gain power legitimately (unlikely, but possible), either get rid of elections or rig them. Dictators have a habit of doing very well in elections they organise: only 169 brave souls voted against Somoza (page 100), apparently disagreeing with 107,000 fellow citizens keen to see him top the poll, while Stroessner (page 120), Mugabe (page 156) and Suharto (page 152) all won dubious 'elections'.

Position yourself as a saviour

Dictators often claim to be the only salvation from some terrible prospect that will destroy the nation, such as Communism, or a dispensable group generally viewed with suspicion, such as the Jews in Germany or the Ugandan Asians. Opponents are then branded as traitors. This gives you licence to deal with them ruthlessly, which leads us to…

Kill, torture, imprison or exile your opponents

A whole set of people will by their nature pose a threat, be it the military, intellectuals, trade unions, a religious group or a rival tribe. Make them suffer: it stops them attacking your position, and is a warning to others who might be tempted into opposition.

Control the media

Free expression provides an avenue for dissent. Stifle any forms of freedom such as the free press, a representative parliament or independent trade unions.

Have a powerful foreign supporter

Isolation often breeds vulnerability, so have at least one powerful foreign supporter. Then you can ignore everybody else. Claim that your country is threatened by a powerful enemy to justify your rule. The US, for example, gladly supported many dictators with appalling records because they were seen as bulwarks against Communism. Foreign support comes in many guises, such as money, weapons or even humanitarian aid, which you can then use to suppress your own people.

Put family members or highly-trusted friends in key positions

A dictator cannot retain power without joining or destroying the old order. You could ingratiate yourself by, say, nationalising foreign-owned industries and handing them over to powerful friends. Or you could boot out the old order, (Peter the Great destroyed the boyar elite and Peron set up a fish market near an exclusive club to show his contempt for the old order). Setting up a new top drawer is a popular move for those at the bottom of the heap, who will smell advancement. Establishing a new elite clique (of which you are the ruler) ensures that the rich and powerful will not plot against you.

Centralise power

Kick out the foreigners you don't need, preferably denouncing them as colonialists. This makes you the champion of the people. Take control of essential industries and the military so that no one can mount a threat. When you are in charge of the economy, others cannot easily build a rival powerbase. If the economic position worsens, buy loyalty by directing all resources to keeping your friends rich (for example, Marcos and

Somoza). They won't mind the nation being impoverished as long as they keep all their trappings.

Start a personality cult
Assign yourself god-like qualities, such as a unique vision of the future (you can even publish your thoughts in a little book, like Mao and Gaddafi). Put up portraits and statues in your honour. Give yourself a title such as 'Only Defender of the People' and get children to recite it at every school assembly. It will help if you have a terrifying reputation for evil-doing, such as voodoo magic ('Papa Doc' Duvalier), cannibalism (Bokassa), cold-blooded murder (Saddam Hussein, Stalin) or horrible violence (Vlad the Impaler).

It will all end in tears
Many dictators become so convinced of their unique value that they make themselves 'President for Life'. The problem with this is that the only way anyone else can achieve power is by killing or exiling you – i.e. doing just what you did to get on the throne. Dictators live in an unreal world, completely out of touch with their own people and often become paranoid: they're (often rightly) afraid someone is going to do to them something similar to what they did to get the keys to the presidential office in the first place. Actually, very few dictators have died in office.

HOW THIS BOOK IS ORGANISED

The dictators are listed in chronological order of birth. Each biography explains their rise, rule and fall, with an insight into their personality and motives, and finally their achievements in historical perspective. Be warned: none of them are very pleasant, but then nice people don't become dictators…

PHEIDON OF ARGOS
(7th century BC)

In a nutshell

Pheidon of Argos was arguably the first dictator in the world. In ancient Greece, tyrant was the term used for a leader who took over power after winning popular support. Pheidon was the first to oust a government by force, and tyrant now means someone who assumes absolute power without the right to it.

Rise and rule

Pheidon had a claim to be the hereditary king of Argos. He consolidated this by building his own army of massed infantry, a relatively new kind of infantry in heavy armour. With this force, he took power and launched a series of offensives against other Greek states, defeating the famous Spartans and overpowering Athens. He also seized control of the Games at Olympia. Pheidon did not allow power to be spread among the nobles and he alone controlled the government.

Downfall

He was apparently killed during a war with Corinth in about 660BC.

What was he like?

Pheidon was a wily operator. When attacking Athens he formed an alliance with the city of Aegina, but when Athens fell he turned his forces on his former ally. On another occasion, he asked the Corinthians for 1,000 young soldiers, supposedly to aid him in war. In fact, he was planning to kill them to weaken the power of Corinth, but the Corinthians detected the plot and refused. He out-fought and out-thought the aristocracy who were accustomed to wielding power.

Today's take

There is considerable dispute about when Pheidon lived, although the Greek writer Aristotle records that he was a king who became a tyrant. Others followed his marching steps and started to take power by military might.

HEROD THE GREAT (c. 73–4BC)

In a nutshell
Immortalised by the story of the census and subsequent infanticide at the time of the birth of Christ, Herod was King of Judea for thirty-two years.

Rise and rule
After his father became Procurator of Judea in 47BC, Herod was made governor of Galilee at the age of twenty-five. He became adept at handling the tricky relationship with Judea's Roman overlords, enlisting their help to put down a rebellion and avenge the murder of his father. Ousted by a Parthian invasion, he persuaded the Romans to back him and took over the Judean crown in 37BC. With victory assured, Herod ordered the massacre of most of Jerusalem in order to establish his authority by terror.

Herod succeeded in juggling the demands of his Jewish subjects (he himself was probably a pagan) with the machinations of Roman politics, helped by his own secret police, which listened for rumours of plots in the marketplace and public baths. He ruled by terror, frequently butchering those who challenged him. For example, he had a group of Jews burned alive for removing the Roman symbolic eagle from the Temple of Jerusalem. Herod also married ten times to create a web of alliances – although being part of his family meant you were at risk from his paranoid fantasies, and he had many close relatives killed, including three sons and one of his wives. He led a major building programme, re-creating Jerusalem after an earthquake and setting up new fortresses. He funded this through new taxes, which were resented by his subjects, partly because he siphoned some of the money away for his own expenditure.

St Matthew's Gospel is the only source for the tale of infanticide for which Herod is notorious: hearing that many Jewish scholars (Pharisees) believed the Messiah was about to be born, he ordered the slaughter of all male infants (estimated at between 10,000 and 150,000), known as the Massacre of the Innocents.

Downfall
Increasingly unstable, Herod attempted suicide but survived. He eventually died in Jericho in c. 4BC.

What was he like?
Herod's success in getting and retaining power was bred from an enormous arrogance and he never blanched from using violence against any perceived threat. He shared the powerful Roman general Marc Antony's love of drinking and feasting.

Today's take

Ruling his kingdom for thirty-two years amidst the whims and plotting of his Roman masters was a major achievement, and Judea flourished during Herod's reign. It only survived for two years after his death, becoming a Roman province at the request of the Jews, who were terrified at the prospect of being ruled by Herod's sons. Parts of the massive temple he had built in Jerusalem survived later Roman attacks, and today form the holy site of the Wailing Wall.

AUGUSTUS CAESAR
(63BC–14AD)

In a nutshell

Also known as Octavian, Augustus Caesar (full name Gaius Julius Caesar Octavianus) combined the ruthlessness of a soldier with the cunning of a politician to become the first, and among the most important, of the Roman emperors.

Rise and rule

Augustus was the great nephew of Roman general Julius Caesar, who famously was killed after being warned to beware the Ides of March. Caesar admired the courage of his nephew, and, with no legitimate children, made him heir to three-quarters of his considerable wealth. At the tender age of eighteen, Octavian formed an uneasy alliance with Marc Antony (who married Octavian's sister) and Marcus Lepidus. This junta, known as the Second Triumvirate, established themselves as the heads of government in 43BC, butchering thousands of enemies on the way.

Marc Antony deserted his wife for the charms of Egypt and its queen Cleopatra, with whom he had already sired three children. Octavian won the backing of the Senate to fight a war against him.

When his main rival committed suicide after a resounding defeat, Octavian then stripped Lepidus of his territories and became the sole Roman ruler. He was given the moniker Augustus, which means 'divine' or 'majestic', and had a month named after him. Knowing that only the army could oust him, he provided land for soldiers who retired, winning their loyalty and weakening his potential enemies. He earned popularity with the people by establishing an honest government and putting on public games.

Keen to avoid the grisly back-stabbing fate of his great uncle, he handled the Senate brilliantly: outwardly respectful but always in command, he took on new roles and titles so that he held the reins of power. This was the beginning of a golden age for the Roman empire after a hundred years of civil war. The system of roads was improved to ease communication throughout the growing empire, and free trade bolstered the economy while art and literature flourished.

Downfall

Augustus was still in power when he died during the month that bears his name, in 14AD. He was pronounced a god a few weeks later.

What was he like?

Augustus was articulate – he gave the oration at his grandmother's funeral when he was just eleven – and a fine soldier. Above all, he was a master at manoeuvring for and holding on to power, and did not hesitate to execute those who posed a threat.

Today's take

Augustus turned the Roman republic into the Roman empire. His legacy was 200 years of peace and prosperity, known as the Pax Romana or the 'Peace of Rome'.

NERO (37–68AD)

In a nutshell

Famously accused of 'fiddling while Rome burned', Nero set new lows with his decadence and casual violence, earning a reputation as one of the most evil tyrants in history, and for killing those closest to him, including his own mother.

Rise and rule

Nero was born into the Roman elite and became emperor in 54AD at the age of seventeen after his uncle was poisoned with mushrooms (an act in which both Nero himself and his mother Agrippina have been implicated). At first, the young ruler was a puppet for his mother, but he tired of her influence and, after several failed attempts at murder using poisons and sabotaging a bedroom ceiling and her boat, he accused her slave of conspiring against him and arranged her supposed 'suicide' in shame.

Numerous others were poisoned or forced into suicide during the fourteen years of his reign and once, in a fit of rage, he kicked a pregnant mistress to death. There was no shortage of plotters against him because of his dissolute life and the corrupt government he ran. Nero was more interested in having affairs with both sexes, fostering the arts and performing on the lyre and in poetry recitals. When Rome suffered a terrible fire in 64AD he is alleged to have watched while playing his favourite instrument – although he is known to have provided shelter and food to survivors. He blamed the fire on the small Christian sect, and had its followers clothed in furs and fed to dogs and lions, or burned in public.

Downfall

It was popularly believed that Nero had arranged the burning of Rome to clear a space large enough for his own grand palace. This suggestion, combined with his scapegoating of Christians who he blamed for the inferno, inspired considerable sympathy for them and loathing for Nero. Desperate to pay for new building works, Nero demanded that wealthy aristocrats promise him money in their wills and then had them murdered. He finally lost the waning confidence of the Senate when he announced that he would defeat some rebels by singing to them. Declared an enemy of the state and condemned to a slave's death of whipping and crucifixion, he took his own life in 68AD.

What was he like?

Nero indulged himself in every way. He gambled and had affairs with women and men in a complex and shifting series of relationships, even having his male lovers castrated to try to turn them into women.

Judges at the public theatrical contests he entered refused him first prize at their own peril.

Today's take
Nero was a popular leader who oversaw long periods of calm prosperity. However, his growing madness and the absence of anyone who could curb his excesses turned his rule to tragedy. He left Rome in a state of crisis and corruption.

WU HOU (625–705)

In a nutshell

Wu Hou (also known as Wu Zetin and Wu Zhao) was
the only female emperor in the history of China.
This remarkable woman was notable for her success
in manipulating herself into power and for her
ruthlessness in disposing of opponents.

Rise and rule

The daughter of a senior official, Wu Hou became one
of the main concubines of Emperor Taizong from 638.
He died in 649, and she should have left the Imperial
Palace for good, but two years later his son Gaozong
brought her back to the harem. They may have already
been having an affair and it is possible she never left.

In a series of manoeuvrings and murders, she got rid
of all her potential rivals, including possibly her own
baby daughter. Gaozong's wife, Wang, was killed by
having her legs and arms broken and being deposited
to die slowly in a large wine urn. Wu Hou became
empress consort in 655, and after her husband suffered
incapacitating strokes in 660 she ruled from behind the
scenes – literally – making decisions from a hidden chair
set behind the throne.

When Gaozong died, she ruled through her two sons,
exiling the first because he was not compliant enough.

She finally had herself crowned Emperor Shengshen in 690, founding the Zhou dynasty. Wu Hou used her own secret police to monitor plots against her, which were brutally suppressed.

Downfall

Unable to thwart the growing plots against her, Wu Hou was ousted by a coup in 705 and died soon after, aged eighty.

What was she like?

Wu Hou had many talents beyond her mastery of intrigue. When young, she was taught to play music, write and read the Chinese classics and her wit and intelligence were renowned. She combated Confucian resistance to female rule by placing women in positions of power and by having biographies of famous women written.

Today's take

Wu Hou was ruthless in her pursuit and tenure of power, but she brought stability to China by improving the system of government and appointing officials through exams, which created a scholarly middle class. She also lowered oppressive taxes, making life better for the Chinese people. Some argue she was no more brutal than her male counterparts, but appears more tenacious because of the perceived weakness of her gender.

GENGHIS KHAN *(c.1162–1227)*

In a nutshell

Genghis Khan built first the Mongol nation (then an enormous empire), gaining control of a huge section of the known world with brute force. He is remembered for the ruthlessness with which this was achieved.

Rise and rule

Born Temüjin Borjigin, he had a tough early life after his clan-leader father was poisoned. Aged about nine, he had the right to take over leadership, but instead the family was banished and had to scavenge to live. When he was twelve, he is reputed to have killed his half-brother Bekhter for stealing some of the family food.

Temüjin slowly gained control of his Mongol clan, and spent about twenty years uniting the other central Asian tribes through a blend of alliances and wars. He eventually built a massive army of about 70,000 men and proceeded to attack the various kingdoms of China from 1211. The nomadic Mongols were accomplished horsemen, but under Genghis they also acquired a huge arsenal of weapons. Fast and lightly armoured, they were highly manoeuvrable, and Genghis was a master military tactician. His army was organised in multiples of ten, each of which elected its own leader, with Genghis in overall command. He would often attack an enemy then retreat to draw them out, before encircling their forces and moving in for the kill.

Genghis Khan was tolerant of other cultures and civilisations provided they bowed the knee to him. Those who refused were attacked and the people who were not enslaved were butchered on a staggering scale and their cities obliterated, creating a climate of terror among his prospective victims. Entire populations were put to the sword, and settlements were ravaged then flooded as the army moved on remorselessly.

Having conquered most of China, by 1223 Genghis Khan had invaded Europe, eventually taking territories as far west as modern Germany. In four years his armies defeated five of the greatest nations in the world to build an empire three times the size of modern North America.

Downfall

Genghis Khan died during or shortly after a battle with the Tangut clan, who had reneged on a promise to join forces with him and so were punished without mercy.

Genghis: the musical

'He was a good husband, a good son and a good friend.'

Dojpalem Ganzorig, lyricist of a popular rock opera about the warlord, which played to cheering groups of Mongolians in 2006.

What was he like?

Genghis Khan was in some ways a benevolent dictator: he allowed his armies to elect their own leaders (under his overall control) and handsomely rewarded his generals for their successes. A strict disciplinarian, he devised a legal code with a fixed penalty for every crime. He was tolerant of other cultures, but not of opposition, which invariably prompted bloodthirsty butchering.

Today's take

It has been estimated that Genghis Khan was responsible for twenty million deaths: about a tenth of the global population at that time. The Mongol expansion continued after his death, following his methods and laws, evidence of how solidly he united a disparate race. Centuries after his death, his name is identified with ruthless expansionism, though in Mongolia itself he is celebrated as a hero.

TIMUR (Tamerlane) *(1336–1405)*

In a nutshell
Timur was a nomadic warlord who never stopped
fighting, building a massive empire in central Asia and
earning an unsurpassed reputation for brutality in
victory.

Rise and rule
Descended from Mongol invaders, possibly including
Genghis Khan (see page 30), Timur earned the
nickname 'Timur the lame' (or Tamerlane) after an
arrow injured his leg, supposedly while he was stealing
sheep. He was a successful military leader in the 1360s,
teaming up with his brother-in-law Amir Husayn to
take over Transoxania (modern-day Uzbekistan).
Showing the zest for violent conflict that permeated
his life, he fell out with Husayn and had him murdered
in 1369.

He spent the next thirty-five years conquering
territories throughout central Asia in a bid to restore
the Mongol empire and plunder as many riches as
he could find. Political commonsense did not come
naturally to Timur, and he often left no government
infrastructure, meaning he regularly had to re-conquer
lands to establish his control for a second time.

He butchered 70,000 in Isfahan during his conquest

of Persia. In 1398, he led the sacking of Delhi in northern India, leaving a mass of ruins and the bodies of more than 50,000 executed captives, their skulls piled into gruesome pyramids. Such was the devastation left behind that it took a hundred years for the city to recover. He invaded Baghdad in 1401, and butchered 20,000 of its citizens.

Downfall

Timur died in 1405 of fever on his way to attack China.

What was he like?

Timur was a brilliant commander but, with little understanding of politics and government and no grasp of delegation, he left a trail of chaos across Asia. A devout Muslim, he showed no mercy to any of his victims, regardless of their faith. He was, however, a patron of art and literature and commissioned the construction of vast public works. Some of the many buildings he constructed still stand today. Timur believed himself to be a direct descendant of Genghis Khan (see page 30) and made it his life's work to try to restore the Mongol empire. In 1941 his tomb

What a legacy

Timur's life was: 'one long story of war, butchery and brutality unsurpassed until the present century'

wrote author **Wilfrid Blunt** in his 1973 text *The Golden Road to Samarkand.*

was exhumed and his facial features were indeed found to be of Mongolian character – and his lameness was also confirmed.

Today's take

Timur was a bandit who roved across a whole continent, conquering but never uniting his territories. The Timurid dynasty, in various forms, survived until 1857.

VLAD THE IMPALER *(1431–1476)*

In a nutshell
Vlad the Impaler ruled the kingdom of Wallachia
in southeast Europe on three separate occasions.
He is best known for his love of impalement and
as the inspiration for the character of Dracula.

Rise and rule
Fifteenth-century Wallachia was caught between two
aggressive neighbours: the Ottoman Empire and the
Kingdom of Hungary. Its insecure crown was not
inherited, but people of noble blood were elected to it
by the boyars. This was clearly a recipe for instability,
and explains in part how Vlad (also known at the time
as Dracula, meaning 'son of Dracul') ruled in 1448, from
1456 to 1462 and again in 1476.

When he was in power he strove to limit the
influence of the nobility, who could get rid of him by
appointing allies to positions of power. He reduced
the economic importance of the nobles and killed
anyone who posed a threat. His favourite among
many cruel and humiliating methods of execution
was impalement: he skewered people in various ways
and left them to die slowly and painfully in public.
The bodies would be left to rot for months, still pinned
to the ground, as a warning to others.

Mass impalements of thousands of people were common and during his rule Vlad killed more of his own people – about 40,000 – than any other ruler until the twentieth century.

Downfall

He was killed after regaining power in 1476 and there are disputes as to how he actually died. However, once he was dead, the Turks decapitated him and sent his head to Constantinople, where it was preserved in honey. The sultan displayed it on a stake, to prove he really was dead.

What was he like?

At the age of eleven, Vlad was sent with his younger brother as a Turkish hostage. His more handsome brother was feted, but the stubborn, unbiddable Vlad witnessed torture, and was subjected to terrible cruelty himself in an underground dungeon, which seems to have warped his personality.

Although he did not invent the idea of impalement, he seems to have become its most devoted practitioner. During a later imprisonment, he captured and skewered birds and mice. Vlad had a strong, if rather twisted, sense of morality and used his favourite punishment on adulterous women, crooked merchants and anyone he decided was lazy (including a woman he chanced across who didn't make her husband's shirts long enough).

Today's take

Vlad's alternative name and elements of his character appear in Bram Stoker's book *Dracula*. The numerous accounts of his sadistic cruelty were exaggerated in tabloid style throughout the Middle Ages, but enough exist from different sources to verify that he was a particularly horrible ruler. Bizarrely, he is apparently something of a folk hero in Romania and Moldova.

IVAN THE TERRIBLE *(1530–1584)*

In a nutshell

Ivan the Terrible is one of the most notorious tyrants in history, famed for his relish of violence and life of depravity.

Rise and rule

Ivan was introduced to the manipulations and deals that surround power from a very early age: he inherited the throne of Russia at the age of three when his father King Vassily III died, but watched others compete for it as he grew up. Isolated, often imprisoned, and generally badly treated by Russia's hereditary nobility, the boyars, he witnessed and was a victim of plots and violence throughout his childhood (including the poisoning of his mother by nobles at court).

By the time he was crowned czar in 1547, he had grown into a sensitive, disturbed, heavy-drinking sixteen-year-old used to seeing opponents sadistically dispatched. His early rule was characterised by modernising reforms that unified his country. However, in 1553, seriously ill with a high fever and fearful that the throne would not be passed to his son Dmitri on his death, he demanded that the boyars swear fidelity to the child. He viewed their reluctant response as treachery and the reprisals he took were immensely brutal.

His instinct for vicious suppression of any threat was tempered by the advice of his first wife, Anastasia, but after her death in 1560, Ivan could not hold back. Taking complete control of the state in 1564, he established Russia's first secret police, the Oprichniki, a black-clad bodyguard sworn to protect him. The Oprichniki spent much of its time killing, torturing or terrorising anyone of whom Ivan disapproved (which frequently included former friends and advisors).

He took a leading part in the Oprichniki's orgies of rape and torture, often ending the debauched sessions with prayers of repentance. Victims were boiled or skinned alive, impaled, blown up on barrels of gunpowder, drowned or simply beaten to death. Ivan himself wielded a metal-tipped staff, not the most reassuring accessory when its owner is subject to wild mood swings. In 1581, he killed his own son with this weapon, apparently by accident, during an argument.

Downfall

Ivan died in 1584, most probably poisoned by his closest advisors with mercury, although he may have been taking it himself to treat his syphilis. Before his death, he was re-christened as a monk called Jonah, and was buried in his monk's habit.

What was he like?

After persecuting animals in his youth (he was known to pitch cats and dogs from high windows of the Kremlin, and to slice open still-twitching birds he had captured), Ivan practised his fascination with sick violence on his own people. He wallowed in the subsequent guilt at his actions, harming himself and leading long prayers of repentance that belied his total lack of compassion for his victims.

Today's take

Ivan the Terrible changed Russia into a multiethnic state by conquering the Tartars and Siberia. He initiated the beginnings of serfdom for the peasantry by restricting their movement, although many of them still abandoned their lands under the terror of the Oprichniki. Admired by Stalin for his ambition and total lack of compromise, he is still regarded as a national hero by many Russians.

PETER THE GREAT (1672–1725)

In a nutshell

Peter the Great is probably the best-regarded of the major dictators because, although he employed the ruthless violence that frequently comes with the role, he also hauled Russia out of the Dark Ages, opened it up to the West and transformed it into a major European power.

Rise and rule

Peter came to the Russian throne at the age of ten, and, caught in a mire of in-fighting, ruled jointly with his half-brother Ivan V, while his half-sister Sophia (who was fifteen years his senior) acted as regent and de facto ruler. For seven years she sat listening and instructing behind a hole specially cut in their two-seater throne.

He was finally able to oust Sophia in 1689, and led a number of military expeditions to establish Russia as a sea power. Peter then embarked on a long trip around western Europe, travelling incognito as part of a group of diplomats. This experience hugely influenced his views, as he saw a world far more developed than backward Russia. He returned in 1698, after Sophia attempted an uprising. She was banished to a convent while her supporters were tortured and killed. Peter himself is said to have participated by beheading some of them.

For the rest of his reign, Peter reorganised and expanded Russia and used its thriving economy to finance wars to regain access to the Baltic Sea and its lucrative trade routes, founding the port of St Petersburg in the process. Not all of his wars were successful and some territories were won and lost after ill-advised expansions. The demands of military campaigns led him to impose conscription to create a million-strong workforce who was put to work building and operating arms factories, military schools, canals and shipyards. He raised money through massive tax rises, punishing protesters with floggings, mutilation, exile or death, and ended the power of the boyar nobles by introducing a new table of ranks based on loyalty to the czar, which lasted until the 1917 revolution. Discovering his eldest son Alexei had plotted against him, he had him tortured and secretly put to death.

Downfall
Peter died still in power in 1725. Mythology has it that he caught a cold after taking part in the rescue of some soldiers drowning in freezing waters near the Finnish Gulf.

What was he like?
Peter was an imposing figure (he was almost seven feet tall) with a dominant and energetic personality to match. He pursued numerous interests and learned many skills such as carpentry (crucial to the building of

the Russian navy). Quick both to anger and laughter, he was fond of using practical jokes to humiliate those he distrusted.

Today's take

Opinion is divided over the value of his legacy. Peter the Great modernised the Russian nation by imposing western ways in many areas of life and government (for example he banned the beards traditionally sported by the boyar elite). While bringing his country into the modern age, he caused enormous suffering by the imposition of heavy taxes and the violent brutality with which opposition was squashed. Some argue that he led Russia to take on a western identity at odds with its previous cultural history. Many Russians still regard him as one of the greatest leaders in their history.

NAPOLEON BONAPARTE
(1769–1821)

In a nutshell

Napoleon changed how wars were fought, and through his victories transformed the map of Europe before he ran out of allies and was overthrown. He is seen as a benevolent dictator because much of his domestic policy modernised, regulated and improved everyday life.

Rise and rule

Napoleon was born in Corsica shortly after it came under French rule. He had to learn French to have schooling and always spoke it with an Italian accent. He joined the army and shot to fame in 1795, when he repelled an armed protest against the revolutionary government in Paris.

Four years later, he was part of a coup that effectively ended the French Revolution and, through his astute manoeuvring, soon made him the most powerful man in France: first consul for life. He put in place a raft of modernising reforms that centralised administration, set up a central bank and introduced codes of law that influenced legal procedures throughout Europe for centuries. However, an assassination plot against him in 1804 inspired him to crown himself as the hereditary emperor, and he subsequently became the dictator of France.

Inside a year, he had claimed the kingship of Italy and annexed Genoa to kick off a decade or so of combat and diplomacy during which he gained control of most of central and eastern Europe before disastrously over-reaching himself by invading Russia. Napoleon was a great commander and a brilliant strategist, who applied the theoretical knowledge gained in his youth to the reality of the battlefield. He broke with tradition by creating a fast-moving, highly-disciplined army in which artillery supported the infantry.

Downfall

Napoleon took 650,000 troops into Russia in 1812, but retreated with less than a tenth of that, and the Russians and Austrians invaded France in 1814. Forced to abdicate to the island of Elba, he returned the following year but was decisively defeated at the Battle of Waterloo in 1815. He was exiled to St Helena Island the same year, and died there six years later.

Important, moi?

Napoleon on himself:

'France has more need of me than I have need of France.'

What was he like?

Napoleon valued education: he applied lessons he had learned in the classroom when directing his forces on the battlefield. He shared a great camaraderie with ordinary soldiers, but also had the vision to direct battles and whole governments. The states he created had efficient administrations which encouraged education, science, literature and the arts.

Today's take

Napoleon redrew the map of Europe and fostered highly influential ideas such as conscription and his codes of law. However, so many of his own people died in his wars that it was decades before France recovered from his rule.

LEOPOLD II OF BELGIUM
(1835–1909)

In a nutshell

Many powerful European states in the nineteenth century were anxious to find a 'place in the sun' and joined the hunt for African colonies. However, King Leopold of Belgium apportioned a chunk of the continent as his own personal fiefdom and treated its people so appallingly that his own state took it from him.

Rise and rule

Leopold was king of Belgium but had no influence on policy. Desperate to cash in on the lucrative exploitation of African territories and unable to convince his own government to do so, in 1879 he commissioned explorer Henry Morton Stanley (who had famously located missionary David Livingstone eight years previously) to find him some land.

Leopold had previously sponsored conferences on protecting Africa's natives from exploitation and guaranteeing free trade. In utterly hypocritical contrast, his instructions to Stanley were to take over the biggest possible area of land and draw up contracts giving exclusive rights to its riches.

As a result Leopold became, in 1885, the personal controller of the Congo Free State (now the Democratic

Republic of Congo), which was seventy-six times the size of Belgium, with a population of thirty million. He never visited it, but he managed to ruin it by decree from a distance of several thousand miles.

He set up his own militia, known as the Force Publique, who exploited the people of Congo by making them produce ivory and rubber for Leopold or his nominated companies (who paid half their profits to the king) for a pittance. Their tactics were persuasive: massacring those who failed to cooperate; enslavement; mass rape; burning down villages; taking women hostage until their men-folk had done the work required. Each village had a quota of how much rubber its people must produce.

A quota was also set for the Force Publique: to stop them wasting ammunition, they had to produce the severed hand of a victim for every bullet they used. Estimates of the number killed vary from five to ten million. Children were taken from their parents and kept in separate camps where they were taught Christianity and how to be soldiers. When the instruction was given that only orphans should receive this treatment, the Force Publique simply shot their parents first.

Writer Joseph Conrad visited the region and described the depraved terror of what he witnessed in his novel *Heart of Darkness*. Also John Harris of Baringa, who was a missionary, was so horrified by what he saw that he wrote a letter to Leopold's chief agent in the Congo: 'The abject misery and utter abandon is positively indescribable. I was so moved, Your Excellency, by the people's stories that I took the liberty of promising them that in future you will only kill them for crimes they commit.'

Downfall

Eventually, the British government issued a report by Roger Casement that shamed the Belgian government into buying the territory from its own king, twenty-three years after he began to ransack it.

What was he like?

Leopold was a wily hypocrite. When pressed on the atrocities done in his name, he commissioned reports from people who owed him allegiance, or lived far apart from one another, and even issued carefully spun, 'positive' summaries of their findings. He scandalised Belgian society by parading his prostitute mistress after his wife's 1902 death.

Today's take

Some of the worst atrocities ever committed in Africa took place in Leopold's name. He remains a controversial figure in the Democratic Republic of Congo: in 2005, a statue of him was removed just hours after being erected in the capital, Kinshasa.

VLADIMIR LENIN (1870–1924)

In a nutshell
One of the most famous revolutionaries in history, Lenin founded the first Communist state and was its leader until his death, after which he became a revolutionary idol.

Rise and rule
Vladimir Ilyich Ulyanov was an active revolutionary from the 1890s, spurred on by the 1887 hanging of his brother Alexander for plotting to kill the czar. He was sent to prison and into exile for a while. Of the many pseudonyms he was forced to adopt, the one that stuck was Lenin, which he used from 1901. He led the Bolsheviks during the 1917 October Revolution, and seized power from the moderate provisional government that had deposed the czar earlier that year.

Lenin set up the Cheka, the Communist secret police, to seek out and punish dissidents during the subsequent three-year civil war, after which Lenin was established at the head of the government. 'Enemies of the revolution', through either class or beliefs, were executed or put into labour camps in a policy of mass terror that Lenin saw as inevitable in the fight against imperialism.

He nationalised banks, private land and other property, and began a policy of controlling food production and distribution, which triggered a famine that starved to death six million Soviet people.

Downfall

In 1922, Lenin was in total control of the country, but his health was failing in part due to a bullet lodged in his shoulder from an attempted assassination in 1918. He suffered a series of strokes, which eventually killed him.

Nice neighbours

Lenin's body was preserved and put on display in a mausoleum in Moscow's Red Square. It is regularly topped up with embalming fluid and any imperfections masked with make-up or wax. Fellow-Soviet dictator Stalin was displayed next to him until he fell from favour and was buried outside the Kremlin walls in 1961.

Hang 'em high

'You need to hang (most definitely hang, so that the public sees) at least one hundred notorious kulaks, the rich, the bloodsuckers.'

Lenin's instructions on quelling rural unrest. Kulaks were rich peasants.

What was he like?

Lenin was a political zealot, a thinker rather than a great public speaker. He disapproved of personality cults and would have despised the way he became the subject of one after his death. He did not shirk the violence he considered necessary to combat capitalism.

Many of his victims were fellow socialists, as a French observer, Charles Rappaport, commented: 'War is declared on anyone who differs with him. Instead of combating his opponents in the Social Democratic Party by Socialist methods, i.e. by argument, Lenin only uses surgical methods, those of bloodletting.'

Today's take

Lenin was revered as a visionary revolutionary for many years, but the collapse of Communism has diminished his reputation recently.

BENITO MUSSOLINI *(1883–1945)*

In a nutshell

Mussolini was an opportunist who exploited the disarray of his country to take power, setting up a ruthlessly violent dictatorship and forming the 'Pact of Steel' with his fellow-Fascist, Hitler.

Rise and rule

After working briefly as a schoolteacher, Mussolini began his political life as a socialist but disagreed with his party's opposition to World War One and left to form his own Fascist party, taking its name from a bundle of rods wrapped around an axe, a symbol of authority in ancient Rome. Backed by his combative Blackshirt

Mussolini's take
'The reign of terror is not a revolution: it is only a necessary instrument in a determined phase of the revolution.'

followers, he exploited Italian unrest and economic upheaval to become King Victor Emmanuel III's choice for a new leader in 1922. He initially worked within the country's nascent democratic structures, but continued tension with socialists led to his sanctioning the assassination of their leader Matteoti in June 1924. After this, Mussolini established a Fascist dictatorship, proclaiming himself Il Duce ('the leader'). He dissolved other parties and insisted that key members of the media and other institutions join his party.

Mussolini followed an aggressive nationalist policy in a bid to build a new Roman Empire. In 1936, he invaded Ethiopia (then known as Abyssinia), using chemical weapons and violent atrocities to establish control. Italy also actively supported fellow-Fascists Franco, in the Spanish Civil War, and Hitler, in Germany.

View from the audience

'An actor extraordinary, with a country for a stage, a great powerful histrionic ego, swaying an audience of millions, confounding the world by his theatrical cleverness.'

George Seldes
in his book
You Can't Print That!

Downfall

After joining World War Two in June 1940, Italy proved to be more of a drain than a support to the Axis powers, and Mussolini, who until then had been safe, even respected, at home and abroad, was relieved of power in 1943. After a brief spell heading a German-supported Fascist state in northern Italy, he was captured and executed, his body suspended upside down next to his mistress in a Milanese square.

What was he like?

Mussolini was a rebellious child, banned from his mother's church for stealing and throwing stones at the worshippers and expelled from school for stabbing another pupil. He was happy to sanction violence to intimidate opponents. A political opportunist, he was very astute in his use of symbolism and understood the Italian need for a sense of nationhood.

Today's take

Mussolini managed to unite a disparate nation through fear and nationalism. However, he dismantled the democratic system that was burgeoning in Italy. The popular saying that at least he made the trains run on time isn't actually true, but he did manage to hold on to power for two decades.

CHIANG KAI-SHEK *(1887–1975)*

In a nutshell

Chiang Kai-shek led China for two decades before losing control to the Communists and retreating to rule the island of Taiwan for a further twenty-six years. He combined a soldier's discipline and ruthlessness with a diplomat's manipulative skills.

Rise and rule

Born into a merchant family but required to work from a young age after his father's death, Chiang Kai-shek began military training at the Paoting Military Academy, before joining the Military State Academy in Japan. He was impressed by the Japanese military's spartan values, and decided that a similarly disciplined force could unify the vast Chinese nation. By now a committed republican, he returned to his homeland to fight the Qing dynasty in 1911. A republic was established and Chiang Kai-shek became a founding member of the nationalist Kuomintang party and fought the emperor's dictatorial replacement. There followed periods spent mixing with the shady Shanghai underworld, fighting for the Kuomintang, being exiled to Japan on a number of occasions and studying the Red Army in Russia.

Shrewd political and military skills enabled him to rise from relative obscurity to lead the Kuomintang (by then governing large tracts of China) in 1925, violently purging it of Communists and forming alliances with regional warlords in a gradual unification of the country. He had assumed sole power over the country by 1936. Chiang Kai-shek's army fought the Japanese invasion of 1937 in a contest that continued through World War Two, in which China took the Allied side after the Japanese bombed Pearl Harbor in 1941. However, Chiang always held back some forces to combat Chinese Communists, who nevertheless eventually succeeded in seizing power in 1949, following three years of civil war.

Chiang Kai-shek fled to the island of Taiwan, where he ruled by martial law, still claiming sovereignty over the whole of China and tacitly supported by the West.

Downfall

Internally, Chiang Kai-shek's strong ties with wealthy landlords had alienated the Chinese peasantry, who regarded him as a corrupt ruler who failed to address China's feudal structure. This was mirrored internationally when the Soviet Union backed Mao Tse-tung's challenge to his leadership, while he became reliant on American support. Chiang Kai-shek died in 1975, still in power in Taiwan.

What was he like?

Chiang Kai-shek maintained the discipline and lack of adornment that so struck him during his time in Japan, but allowed corruption to flourish elsewhere. He held his own amongst major international personalities such as Stalin, Roosevelt and Churchill, and was adept at forming alliances to reinforce his position.

Today's take

Chiang Kai-shek did much to unify China, but crucially failed to win over the peasantry. He left Taiwan economically vibrant and his son helped transform it into a genuine democracy.

JOSEF STALIN (1879–1953)

In a nutshell

Josef Stalin was one of the most feared figures of the twentieth century – by the international community and especially by his fellow countrymen. While working towards making the USSR a superpower, he was responsible for the deaths of many millions of people. He changed his name in 1913 to Stalin, the Russian term for 'Man of Steel'.

Rise and rule

Stalin built up a power base as general secretary of the Communist Party and was already notorious for his use of violence when he took over power following the death of Lenin in 1924.

'A sincere diplomat is like dry water or wooden iron.'

Joseph Stalin

In 1934 the assassination of a popular colleague of Stalin's, Sergey Kirov, led to a massive purge of the Old Bolshevik order. Some believe Stalin himself ordered the killing, but there is no evidence of this. What is certain is that over the next few years thousands of formerly high-ranking revolutionaries were executed, sometimes after show trials. Fellow revolutionary leader Leon Trotsky claimed that Stalin's regime was now separated from that of Lenin by a 'river of blood' – and was himself killed on Stalin's orders in 1940. Stalin also reinstated the gulags – slave camps where dissidents or those with individualistic tendencies were forced to work for nothing in barbaric conditions. He introduced a policy of collectivisation, taking over farms to make them more efficient while tightening the state's grip on the peasant farmers. Any resistance was a death warrant. Stalin's rule extended into the arts and culture: from 1932 all artists were required to follow the state policy of 'Socialist realism' in their work, abandoning 'decadent' or 'bourgeois' trends such as impressionism and cubism. As a result, people such as artists, writers and musicians

Some mistakes are bigger than others

'Everyone can err, but Stalin considered that he never erred, that he was always right. He never acknowledged to anyone that he made any mistake, large or small, despite the fact that he made not a few mistakes in the matter of theory and in his practical activity.'

Soviet Union premier **Nikita Krushchev**, 1956.

lived in fear that Stalin would pronounce their work as counter-revolutionary and end their careers with a one-way trip to the gulags.

Shunned by the appalled Western nations, Stalin negotiated a non-aggression pact with Nazi Germany, which was betrayed when his fellow-dictator Hitler attacked the Soviet Union in 1941. German successes were eventually countered by sacrificing millions of poorly-equipped and ill-trained Russian troops, who knew that desertion or surrender meant punishment with a bullet or the gulags. Stalin took all the credit for the victory.

He then succeeded in forcing Communist regimes onto most of eastern Europe, providing him with a powerbase from which the Soviet Union emerged as a superpower and rival to the United States.

Downfall

Stalin stayed in power until he died, still ruthlessly purging any sign of dissent. When he suffered a stroke during the night of 5 March 1953, his guards were too frightened to enter his room until the next evening, and he died a few days later.

What was he like?

Stalin came from peasant stock and although he did well at school he was mocked for his Georgian accent. His father was often absent or drunk and frequently beat his son. Childhood friends commented that this treatment hardened the boy never to show his feelings and to hate authority. Such was Stalin's lack of emotion that he let his own son perish in a Nazi concentration camp, despite being given the opportunity to release him in exchange for a German general held by the Russians. He is reported to have said: 'A lieutenant is not worth a general.'

He established an image as a patriotic leader and such was the extent of his personality cult that he even had his name included in the Soviet national anthem. Other politicians reluctantly admired his uncompromising approach to negotiation. Stalin took a ghoulish interest in precisely how the victims he selected for torture had died.

'Ideas are more powerful than guns. We would not let our enemies have guns, why should we let them have ideas?'

Josef Stalin

Today's take

There is no doubt that Stalin established the Soviet Union as a major world power. There were massive improvements in the provision of medical care and education during his reign, and some argue he showed great leadership during World War Two. But he ruled through absolute fear, inflicting suffering and death on an unimaginable scale. The death toll of his own people during his reign is thought to have been between twenty and thirty million.

The collapse of the Soviet Union and of many Communist regimes in eastern Europe was partly caused by enormous resentment at a brutal central government and intolerance of ethnic culture. 'Stalinism' has become a synonym for state terror.

ADOLF HITLER (1889–1945)

In a nutshell

Adolf Hitler was one of the most evil men of the twentieth century. He approved the mass murder of up to six million Jews alone, having provoked a global conflict that killed perhaps ten times that figure. His policies of hatred, persecution and war destroyed the country he claimed to love.

Rise and rule

Born in Austria, Hitler left school with no qualifications, and his teachers commented that he showed no desire to work. Partly supported by family money, he scratched a living as an undistinguished artist.

'I intend to set up a thousand-year Reich and anyone who supports me in this battle is a fellow-fighter for a unique spiritual – I would say divine – creation.'

Adolf Hitler

He joined the army in World War One and earned the Iron Cross medal, among others, for bravery, and was wounded several times. However, he only achieved the rank of corporal as he apparently lacked leadership skills. He enjoyed military life and stayed on in the army as a political agent, joining the nationalist

German Workers' Party (soon renamed the National Socialist German Workers' Party, or NSDAP), where he was put in charge of propaganda in 1920. There was already a strand of anti-Semitism in German politics and the National Socialists reflected this, together with a hatred of Communism, backing it up with violent thuggery on the streets.

Hitler was jailed for his part in a failed coup in 1923 (the Munich, or Beer Hall, Putsch), and while in prison wrote a self-serving book describing his philosophy, called *Mein Kampf* ('My Struggle').

My brother, the devil

'I would have preferred it if he'd followed his original ambition and become an architect.'

Adolf Hitler's much younger sister, Paula, interviewed towards the end of 1945.

Economic difficulties, such as the Depression of 1929, and a lingering resentment at the humiliating settlement imposed on Germany after World War One (the Treaty of Versailles) created the right climate for nationalist rhetoric that blamed non-Germans for the country's travails.

An alliance with another nationalist group brought the party a higher profile and more seats, and Hitler was eventually appointed chancellor in 1933.

When President von Hindenberg died the following year, Hitler merged the two offices and took over the army. He had already effectively banned other parties and set up the Gestapo secret police. He then stripped Jews of German citizenship, sending many into exile, and established concentration camps for them and other 'unwanted' groups such as the handicapped and dissidents.

Friends in high places
'Silence, indifference and inaction were Hitler's principal allies.'

Chief Rabbi Baron Immanuel Jakobovits
speaking in 1989.

Hitler built up the army, introduced conscription and began his expansionist plans by claiming Austria and the Sudetenland (part of the former Czechoslovakia) as German territory. The main Western powers followed an appeasement policy of trying to accommodate these demands, giving Hitler the confidence to invade the rest of Czechoslovakia and then Poland in 1939. This finally provoked war in Europe.

Initial success in World War Two was stymied by many factors: first, a failure to gain control over Britain or North Africa; second, Hitler's decision to break the non-aggression pact and invade Russia in 1941; and third, the entry of the US to the war the same year.

While this protracted and bloody war was going on, Hitler approved the 'Final Solution'. Concentration camps were transformed into killing camps for millions of Jews along with gypsies, homosexuals, Slavs, the disabled and other groups deigned to be inferior. Many were worked to death; others died from maltreatment or disease, or were gassed to death. The total number of people killed in this Holocaust is believed to be 11 million, including 6 million Jews.

Downfall

Hitler committed suicide, along with his new wife, Eva Braun, in his Berlin bunker, as Soviet troops closed in on the capital on 29 April 1945.

What was he like?

Hitler's father was a violent man, and as a child Adolf felt unable to protect his mother. He was a lonely figure living in a fantasy world, and he owed much of his success to his mesmeric public speaking – he was a poor writer (*Mein Kampf* was ghost-written by Rudolf Hess). Hitler was prone to paranoid temper tantrums, which may have been exacerbated by the cocktail of drugs he was prescribed for various ailments.

'Every word that comes from Hitler's mouth is a lie. When he says peace, he means war, and when he blasphemously uses the name of the Almighty, he means the power of evil, the fallen angel, Satan.'

Winston Churchill

Today's take

Hitler showed that propaganda, a gift for speaking at large demonstrations and exploiting people's fears and prejudices can bring a demagogue to power. While he manipulated Germany's yearning for national pride, Hitler did not share his fellow-Fascist Mussolini's interest in domestic policy, and he must be judged more on his war-mongering and racist policies. His legacy was infamy for the enormous evil he unleashed on the world.

RAFAEL LEÓNIDAS TRUJILLO
(1891–1961)

In a nutshell
Rafael Leónidas Trujillo ruled the Dominican Republic for thirty-one years from 1930, running the country as a family business and torturing and killing those who opposed him or were unlucky enough to have the wrong colour skin, in his opinion.

Rise and rule
Trained by the US Marines during the American occupation of his country, Trujillo became the army chief, from where he ousted President Horacio Vásquez in 1930. He ruled until 1961, sometimes with the title of president (1930–38, 1942–52). He was able to stay in power because foreign governments approved of his anti-Communist stance and a fearful populace saw the ruthless treatment meted out to opponents – although they were also given the chance to vote for Trujillo's Partido Dominciano in several elections (in which no other candidates participated).

One policy he pursued, called *blanquismo*, aimed to increase the number of white-skinned people in his mixed-race country (the dictator apparently whitened his own slightly dark complexion with make-up).

In 1937, he sanctioned the genocide of up to 20,000 sugar cane workers (men, women and children) living near the border with Haiti, killing only those with French, rather than Spanish accents. He gained international attention when, in the 1930s, he began welcoming Jewish refugees, while other more affluent countries were turning them away. Whether this was a humanitarian gesture or an intelligent public relations ploy is still a matter of debate.

Under his iron rule, the quantity of imported goods was reduced and the economy thrived, often to Trujillo's personal advantage – he bought and sold nationalised industries as he pleased. All foreign debt was repaid, and there were many public building and works projects and a rise in education standards.

Downfall

Trujillo was suspected of organising the disappearance of an exiled academic critic, Jesús de Galíndez, who was kidnapped from New York in 1956 and never seen again. Scandals such as this, and his continued meddling in the affairs of fellow Caribbean states, led other powers to wish for a less aggressively reactionary government in the Dominican Republic. On 30 May 1961, Trujillo was shot down in his car by some of his own troops, allegedly armed by the CIA.

What was he like?

Trujillo ran his own personality cult, rechristening a city and a mountain in his name, while schoolchildren were expected to pray for him. He took the wives of colleagues as his mistresses, and devised some particularly barbaric methods of torture.

Today's take

One of the benefits of Trujillo tying his fortunes so closely with those of the Dominican economy was that the country's finances stayed in fairly good shape throughout his rule. The downside was a public terrorised by his repressive personality cult, his secret police and the fearsome violence he unleashed on any opposition.

FRANCISCO FRANCO
(1892–1975)

In a nutshell
Franco ranks as one of the most 'successful' dictators of modern times, staying in power for thirty-six years as Spain's de facto king. His country was isolated from the rest of the world for part of his reign due to his violent repression of opposition as he attempted to bring stability to Spain – at a price measured in hundreds of thousands of lives.

Rise and rule
Franco was a successful soldier with a reputation as a strict disciplinarian who was skilled in battle. He became the army's youngest general and from 1935 held its senior post: chief of the general staff.

The following year, at a time of great political instability, the military tried to take over, sparking the Spanish Civil War between the Nationalists and the Republicans. Franco played a key role in this contest, forging close links with the right wing-regimes in Italy and especially Germany (which was responsible for the carpet-bombing of the undefended Basque town of Guernica, one of numerous atrocities committed by both sides in the three-year war).

The victorious Nationalists made Franco head of

state and he imposed martial law until 1948, continuing to execute his opponents, outlawing other parties, banning strikes, and binding the Catholic Church to his regime by giving it

Telling it like it is
'Our regime is based on bayonets and blood, not on hypocritical elections.'

control of education and stopping civil marriage. It is estimated that 200,000 political prisoners died from starvation, overwork and execution.

During World War Two, Franco maintained Spain's neutrality (though he was pressured often by Hitler to join the Axis powers); he did, however, provide Germany with logistical and intelligence support. After the war Spain was an international pariah, until Franco's strong anti-Communism proved useful to the West during the Cold War: Spain was rehabilitated, joining the United Nations in 1955. Franco oversaw an upsurge in the Spanish economy when he replaced military administrators with civilian businessmen from 1957, but this did little to revive his popularity and a rise in dissidence led to a repressive clampdown in 1969.

Downfall

Amid rising discontent, Franco died still holding on to power in 1975. He had already appointed Juan Carlos as his successor in a re-established monarchy. Though many believed the king, groomed by Franco himself, would follow in the dictator's footsteps, in fact he worked with politicians and labour groups to bring democracy back to Spain.

What was he like?

Franco did not have strong political views, except hating Communism, and his policy was to bring stability and discipline. An avowed monarchist, he adopted the linguistic and lifestyle trappings of the king he clearly wished to be. In the army, he severely punished minor misdeeds, and in power he was willing to torture or kill any of his fellow countrymen who opposed his regime. His ready use of violence reflected the aggression of his alcoholic father, which he witnessed in his youth.

Today's take

Spain returned to democracy within three years of Franco's death, and his reputation as a strong, uniting leader has been undermined by acknowledgement of the atrocities he sanctioned. He was largely responsible for preventing Communist rule in Spain, and for keeping his country out of World War Two. Spain's economic prosperity was bought at the price of thousands of deaths together with the repression of liberal ideas and independent-thinking groups such as trade unions, the clergy and the Basques.

MAO ZEDONG *(1893–1976)*

In a nutshell
Mao Zedong exerted an extraordinary influence over his country for twenty-five years, fuelled by a dogma through which he tried to control not only what people did, but what they thought.

Rise and rule

Power source

'Political power grows out of the barrel of a gun.'

Mao, 1939.

Although he was of peasant stock, Mao's family was fairly prosperous and he was extremely well educated; he was widely read and had a great admiration for Napoleon and George Washington, as well as for Chinese culture. Mao was a teacher and an activist, embracing Marxism-Leninism and quickly becoming disillusioned with the pragmatic wheeling and dealing of China's Kuomintang leader Chiang Kai-shek (see page 66).

China was emerging from its imperial feudal structure, and Mao realised that the millions of rural workers, resentful of their powerful landlords, were more ripe for revolution than their urban counterparts. He founded a group of peasant guerrillas who were to become the Red Army, and battled with government forces until joining them to fight the Japanese in World War Two. He pursued a civil war from 1945, backed by the Soviet Union, and on 1 October 1949 proclaimed a new People's Republic of China in Beijing's Tiananmen Square.

China's innumerable small farms were transformed into communes which were set quotas on what to produce through a series of Five Year Plans. The second and most famous – infamous – of these was the Great Leap Forward begun in 1958. This plan reflected Mao's determination to make China a major grain and steel producer, despite the country's lack of skills in the latter industry.

Mao wanted to make use of China's enormous population by using cheap labour rather than expensive imported machinery. Therefore much of the countryside was re-organised into people's communes which were to carry out industrial work as well as agriculture. Since they lacked the skills and resources to achieve this, the Great Leap Forward actually resulted in a gigantic leap backwards with the virtual collapse of the economy.

Part of the problem was that Mao did not trust experts to guide him, so made decisions based on his own imperfect understanding of industry. No-one dared challenge him for fear of being 're-educated' out of this negative viewpoint, and indeed officials provided inflated figures of production to escape the wrath of Mao and his quota system.

The blinkered insanity of Mao's dogmatic approach is illustrated by the 1958 edict that for one day everyone should bash pots and pans to terrify to death the sparrows which were eating the people's crops.

For the next two years insects relieved of their predators munched their way through fields which were already suffering from droughts, floods and mismanagement in what may be the biggest famine in history.

In the Cultural Revolution of 1966-68, Mao created a climate in which children willingly denounced their parents as bourgeois anti-revolutionaries and where to be an intellectual was the sign of a traitor. About three million who expressed opposition to him were executed, while millions more were 're-educated' by being sent to toil in the fields and attend lectures on their leader's beliefs. His major weapon in the Cultural Revolution was the Red Guards, which mainly

Smile!

Mao followed the peasant custom of rinsing his teeth in green tea every day, commenting that 'a tiger never brushes his teeth'. Consequently, they turned the colour of his tea (not helped by his three-pack-a day smoking habit) and nearly all of them had fallen out by the end of his life.

comprised students recruited to ensure his own brand of Communism was not diluted by rivals within his own party. They created a climate in which only Mao's thoughts had validity. Mao became one of the richest men in the country from sales of the famous 'Little Red Book' of his sayings, culled from his speeches and published in 1964 as part of a massive and hugely successful personality cult.

'There are different types of intellectuals in China. Engineers and technicians are more receptive to socialism. Scientists are next. Those who study liberal arts are the worst.'

Downfall

Mao died in 1976 at the age of eighty-two, still in power and with no clear successor.

What was he like?

A professed enemy of individuality, Mao established a personality cult that identified him totally with China. He showed extraordinary courage and stoicism in his march to power, and was a master of the political plot. He knew China's history and saw himself as an emperor forcing his people to make sacrifices for the common good. Away from the view of the people, he was a compulsive womaniser with a huge collection of pornography.

Today's take

Mao's rule was a triumph of dogma over experience, and by the time he died the country could barely feed itself, and its people lived in fear of their leader and of each other. China became isolated internationally, although Mao had stunned the world in 1972 by meeting with US President Richard Nixon, paving the way for China to join the United Nations Security Council. His main achievement was arguably the feat of seizing and holding on to power in a country covering more than nine million square kilometres with a one billion-plus population.

JUAN PERÓN (1895–1974)

In a nutshell

Was Juan Perón a dictator? Some historians dispute it, pointing out that he was legitimately elected to office three times. However, many agree that his repressive and violent methods once in charge merit him a place on the list.

Rise and rule

Juan Perón served as Argentina's military attaché in Mussolini's Italy, and used some of the Fascist dictator's methods later in his life. He was instrumental in Argentina's 1943 military coup, and served in the resulting new government as secretary of labour and welfare. Reforms he instigated won him the popular support of the poor workers (*descamisados*, or 'shirtless ones'). This was vital in earning him a release from prison after a rival military group took over, and he then was elected president in February 1946, with fifty-six per cent of the vote.

During his first term, Perón waged a campaign against universities and students; a popular slogan at the time, which appeared on many posters, was:

'Build the Fatherland. Kill a Student'.

Perón followed what he called the 'third position': enlightened nationalist policies somewhere between Communism and capitalism, encouraging industrialisation and expanding the role of the unions. Argentina became a major wheat and beef exporter, increasing its prosperity, and Perón was also able to draw on the considerable government reserves – achieved from exports in World War Two – to fund new social housing, widen the availability of education and improve the infrastructure of Argentina.

These popular policies were supplemented by repressive violence toward enemies, something he had witnessed in 1930s Italy. He had by now married his second wife, Eva, widely known as Evita, a glamorous and popular figure who is credited with many of his pro-labour and -women policies, and the couple were regarded as pseudo-royalty.

Downfall

Economic downturns, corruption and conflict with the powerful Catholic Church led to Perón being ousted by a military coup in 1955. However, volatile Argentinian politics brought his return from Spanish exile and re-election as president in 1973. During this period he used a series of emergency decrees and military actions to combat terrorist attacks. Inflation raged, however, and he had not restored stability by the time he died in July 1974.

What was he like?

Perón was a mass of contradictions: he was a Fascist sympathiser who pursued enlightened social policies, and he was closely identified with repression and corruption.

Today's take

His political standpoint had a huge impact on the life and politics of Argentina, and Perón's glamorous profile, aided by a trio of influential wives, made him a unique and charismatic figure. Perón's progressive policies improved everyday life for his people, but his use of thugs against his opponents did not bring order to the often-unstable politics of his country.

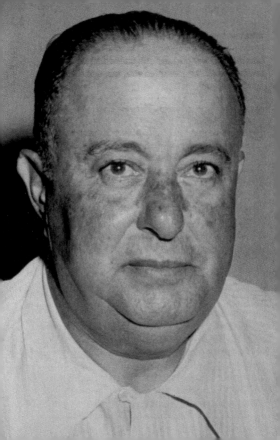

ANASTASIO SOMOZA GARCÍA *(1896–1956)*

In a nutshell
The Somoza family gained power in Nicaragua by violence and kept it through rigged elections and puppet regimes with the help of generous support from the US. While in power they plundered their country's resources to bank a multi-million dollar fortune.

Rise and rule
Somoza spent his teenage years in Philadelphia, gaining a deep understanding of American culture and losing his native accent. Both were to prove useful in his rise to power. The US Marines had entered Nicaragua in 1912 and spent twenty years fighting revolutionaries to protect American business interests. Somoza worked as a translator and a soldier in the US-organised National Guard. In 1934, while negotiating peace terms with the revolutionary Augusto Sandino, Somoza ordered the assassination of his opponent, violating an agreed truce. He continued to interfere in politics for the next two years and was elected president in 1936, immediately changing the constitution to give him total power and installing family members in key posts.

The National Guard killed off Sandino's followers and other dissidents, and Somoza confiscated their land, adding to it a portfolio of valuable properties and investments granted at low prices. Within ten years he was the largest landowner in Nicaragua, and was also taking 'commissions' from international (mainly US) gold, rubber and timber companies. If there was a kickback to be had or a deal to force, he took advantage, acquiring a colossal dollar fortune. He also gained control of all government and national radio and telegraph services, and set up a select group of enforcers known as the 'blue shirts'.

Downfall

The US tolerated all this because of his opposition to Communism. One of Franklin D. Roosevelt's staff famously commented to the US president that 'Somoza may be a son of a bitch, but he's our son of a bitch'. However, Somoza became an embarrassment, and in 1944 the US told him not to stand for re-election. He put up a nominee, Leonardo Arguello, as his puppet in a rigged election but Arguello cut the strings and tried to restrict the National Guard so Somoza orchestrated a coup and installed his wife's uncle as president. A year after getting himself re-elected as president in 1955, Somoza was shot on a León street. He died several days later.

His sons succeeded him; first (briefly) Luis, then Anastasio Jnr. who retained the Somozas' grip on

Nicaragua, sometimes through figureheads, for another twenty-four years, ruling in a similar style to his father. An example of the cynical exploitation of the Nicaraguan people was the illegal taking and running of international relief aid after the 1972 earthquake in the capital Managua.

What was he like?
Somoza was greedy, corrupt and deceitful. He showed total contempt for democratic and legal processes, taking and doing what he wanted by threatening force.

Today's take
While the Nicaraguan economy initially prospered under Anastasio Somoza García (to his particular benefit), the country became totally dependent on the US and virtually collapsed in 1954. His family continued to plunder the land throughout their time in power, and the Somoza name has become synonymous with unbridled corruption.

HASTINGS KAMUZU BANDA
(c. 1898–1997)

In a nutshell

Hastings Banda is that rare thing: a dictator still revered (and possibly feared) by many of his people. He returned from abroad to lead his country to independence and ruled it for over thirty years.

Rise and rule

Banda came from a peasant background in what was then the British protectorate of Nyasaland, and was heavily influenced by Scottish Presbyterian missionaries. Medical training in the US and Britain led to work as a doctor in Scotland and England.

He returned to his homeland in 1958 to help in the battle for independence. He became a national figure and the natural choice as the first prime minister of the new nation of Malawi (a name Banda himself chose) in 1963. He became president three years later when he declared a one-party state. Given his stern autocratic manner, it was a natural step for him to declare himself president for life in 1971.

His allies characterised his rule as paternalistic. His enemies called him a dictator. Certainly power was centred on him: he headed the ministries of Agriculture, Justice, Information, Tourism, Works,

Foreign Affairs and Defence. No dissent was tolerated, and rival political leaders were exiled or killed if they posed enough of a threat. Some aspects of his rule were enlightened: the country gained an infrastructure of new roads, airports, hospitals and schools, and Banda founded an institution to recognise and improve women's rights in Malawi.

Banda had little time for other African leaders, and Malawi was the only state to maintain relations with the generally despised South Africa during its apartheid years. His pro-Western stance was symbolised by his English-style dark three-piece suits with matching handkerchiefs, and a black homburg hat.

Banda built a huge personal fortune, estimated at nearly US$320 million, at a time when more than half his people lived below the poverty line.

Downfall

Domestic unrest and international pressure forced Banda to signal the end of his thirty-year rule by calling a referendum on whether to have a multi-party democracy in 1993, and he was voted out the following year. In 1995, he was cleared of charges of assassinating four political opponents and he died two years later, being buried in a $50,000 gold-plated coffin.

What was he like?

Banda enjoyed the trappings of power: his citizens were expected to applaud in the streets as he was driven past in his Rolls Royce convertible on his way to a $100 million palace in the capital of Lilongwe. His Presbyterian and medical background are unusual for a dictator, but he was a fiery nationalist who saw himself as essential to the survival of his country.

Today's take

Malawi remains an impoverished country, now riven by AIDS. Its shops are still stocked with cassettes and videotapes of the speeches, and especially the spectacular funeral, of its founding leader.

FRANÇOIS 'PAPA DOC' DUVALIER *(1907–1971)*

In a nutshell

François Duvalier transformed himself from a country doctor to an international shyster in the space of a few years. Exploiting the US fear of Cuba and Communism, he built a multi-million dollar fortune at the expense of the starving people of Haiti, whom he encouraged to believe in his supernatural voodoo powers.

Rise and rule

François Duvalier trained and worked as a doctor (hence his later nickname) before becoming minister of health and labour. During this time, he had observed the repressive methods of Haitian politicians and studied the Haitian voodoo religion. In 1957, he was voted in as president following an election rigged by the military who probably thought this timid country doctor would serve as their puppet.

Duvalier, however, transformed himself. In addition to his Presidential Guard, he set up his own militia, the Tontons Macoutes. Their name derives from a Creole term for a bogeyman (*tonton* meaning 'uncle' and *macoutes* meaning 'gunnysack'), who takes people in the night and makes them disappear forever, which is exactly what they did. This unsalaried force (they relied on extortion and corruption) had more power in Haiti than the newly slimmed-down army, and it served as Duvalier's power base while he consolidated his hold on government against a divided opposition. His enemies were sent to the notorious Fort Dimanche to be tortured, usually to death.

He exploited the popular mysticism that was part of Haitian culture by posing in pictures wearing the top hat and tails of Baron Samedi, the voodoo spirit of the dead.

Duvalier was adept at exploiting the US's fear of Communism, and of nearby Castro's Cuba, wrangling enormous amounts of monetary aid, which was instantly siphoned off into his own bank account. His main foreign policy strategy was flattery, and he particularly relished issuing medals of honour to dignitaries in return for 'loans'. Many of these were supposedly to fund the utopian town of Duvalierville, which was never built.

Downfall

As the economy collapsed and the middle classes fled, 'Papa Doc' declared himself president for life in 1964. A few months before he died in 1971 he installed his son in power, who kept the family in power for a further fifteen years.

What was he like?

As a doctor, Duvalier participated in a US-funded blitz on yaws (a crippling bacterial disease), later presenting himself as its single-handed defeater. He was pictured apparently receiving the blessing of Jesus Christ and even issued a revised Lord's Prayer that began 'Our Doc, who art in the National Palace for life…'

Today's take

Duvalier wreaked havoc on Haiti, crippling the economy and creating millions of political and economic refugees. He gained notoriety for establishing one of the vilest dictatorships of modern times.

NE WIN *(1911–2002)*

In a nutshell

Ne Win cut off Burma (known as Myanmar since 1988) from the rest of the world as he attempted to impose a system combining Marxism and Buddhism on his country. The result was economic chaos.

Rise and rule

British withdrawal in 1948 left the newly independent Burma in turmoil. Ne Win's key role in the military and in several government posts enabled him to help hold the nation together. In 1962, two years after losing power through democratic elections, Ne Win led a bloodless coup, arresting key ministers and representatives of rival ethnic groups. He established a one-party state in which he ruled by decree, following his self-proclaimed 'Burmese path to Socialism', which turned out to be a road to ruin. Foreign businesses were forced out and all private enterprise nationalised, creating a chaotic and corrupt economy in which people were forced to get food on the black market. Once the world's major rice exporter, Burma's economy went into reverse and the country became isolated from the rest of the world (foreigners were only allowed in on 3-day visas).

Internal dissent was violently crushed, for example student demonstrations in Rangoon in 1962 saw a hundred unarmed protesters shot dead and the university's student union building dynamited. In 1974 food shortages caused riots which were callously put down and Ne Win declared martial law.

Downfall

Ne Win announced his retirement on 8th August 1988 – a date the numerology-obsessed leader believed had auspicious meaning (8.8.88). Four days of pro-democracy demonstrations saw up to ten thousand demonstrators injured or killed by troops and the successors he had chosen put the main focus of opposition, Aung San Suu Kyi, under house arrest for seven years.

Ne Win remained a shadowy figure behind the new military government until 1998 after which he became marginalised. He was accused of involvement in a plot to seize power by some of his grandchildren. When he died in 2002 the Burmese media did not cover his death and no members of the government attended his funeral.

What was he like?

Originally called Shu Maung, in 1941 he adopted the name Ne Win because it means 'brilliant as the sun', indicative of his huge ego. Ne Win was a drinker and a gambler, and he had a cruel streak – he is alleged to have beaten a colleague to death with a golf club. An obsession with numerology (belief in the significance of certain numbers) led him to reissue Burma's banknotes in new denominations, causing economic havoc. He was said to have bathed in dolphin's blood in an attempt to regain his youth.

Today's take

Ne Win's military leadership probably stopped Burma from breaking up on ethnic lines in 1948, but his subsequent 'Path to Socialism' took Burma from relative prosperity to a place on the United Nations' list of the ten poorest nations in the world.

KIM IL-SUNG *(1912–1994)*

In a nutshell

Kim Il-sung perhaps came closest of any dictator to turning himself into a god during his forty-six-year-rule. He led his people into war and starvation, but his death prompted an enormous display of public mourning.

Rise and rule

Kim Il-sung's family fled to China when he was eight to escape the Japanese occupation of Korea. Ten years later, in 1930, he joined the fight against the hated oppressors, later changing his name to Kim Il-sung, meaning 'become the sun', showing an early grasp of the value of public relations.

The Japanese occupation did not survive World War Two, and in 1945 Korea was divided into South and North Korea, backed by the US and USSR respectively. Kim Il-sung had trained and worked with the Soviet authorities (becoming a captain in the Red Guard) and in 1948 they installed him in North Korea as leader of the new regime (the Democratic People's Republic of Korea), whereupon he put his old guerrilla comrades into key positions. His government introduced a series of reforms including Soviet-style collectivisation of and and nationalisation of heavy industry, particularly arms production.

Now, the cult of Kim (known as the Great Leader) became all-important: all North Koreans had to wear a lapel pin with his photograph over their hearts and display his picture in their homes. Statues in his image appeared all over the country and it was claimed that the sun rose on his command.

Kim made the mistake of alienating the USSR, which then withdrew its support from the war-based economy. Foreigners were excluded from large parts of the country, where the population came near to starvation and street executions for minor offences were a terrifying reminder of the dangers of non-conformity. Kim followed a policy of *Juche* (self-reliance) and the huge decrease in foreign trade led to significant food shortages in the country, which are still prevalent today.

Downfall
Kim Il-sung groomed his son Kim Jong-il (see page 180) to succeed him, which he did after his father's death in 1994.

What was he like?
Kim operated a nauseating personality cult in a bid to depict himself to his people as a near-god. A three-year 'official mourning' period was imposed after his death, and during this time North Koreans could be punished for not mourning sufficiently.

Today's take
Kim Il-sung was adept at playing his Soviet and Chinese backers against each other, but when they withdrew funding, his insistence on a military-based, inward-facing economy resulted in many of his people struggling to put food in their mouths. The collapse of the USSR only served to increase the international isolation of his country, in marked contrast to US-backed South Korea.

ALFREDO STROESSNER
(1912–2006)

In a nutshell

Alfredo Stroessner was the archetypal South American dictator: a Communist-hating strongman in a gold-braided military uniform, who offered a safe haven for Nazis on the run while arranging the 'disappearance' of his opponents.

Rise and rule

After backing a series of successful military coups from his senior position in the army, Stroessner did the obvious thing and staged one of his own in 1954 to usurp Frederic Chavez. He proceeded to rule for the next thirty-five years, winning eight consecutive presidential elections … as the only candidate.

His fervent anti-Communism ensured support from the US, whose military aid helped the army to ruthlessly suppress dissident groups. Enemies faced torture and terminal kidnapping, with some being thrown to their death from aeroplanes or bound and fed to the piranha fish in the Río Paraguay. At times Stroessner showed signs of loosening his grip and allowing liberal reforms, probably in a bid to stay on as president for life.

Downfall

Stroessner conformed to the previous pattern of Paraguayan politics, being overthrown by a military coup in 1989. By this time, his regime had lost American support because of its violent excesses. Exiled to Brazil, he resisted attempts to extradite him and charge him with human rights abuses until his death in 2006.

What was he like?

Born to an immigrant German father and a Paraguayan mother, Stroessner grew up to become a brave soldier who inspired loyalty in his troops. Once in power, he was a diligent dictator: he never took a holiday and was at his desk from six o'clock in the morning until late at night – although he allowed himself a three-hour siesta.

Dial S for murder

In 1975, the secretary of the Paraguayan Communist Party, Miguel Soler, was ripped apart with a chain saw during a torture session attended by Stroessner's favourite sadist, Pastor Coronel, while his master listened in down a telephone line.

Today's take

Stroessner pursued an austere economic policy that boosted exports and investment, greatly benefiting the Paraguayan economy. Harbouring the notorious Nazi doctor Josef Mengele, and about 300 other Nazis after World War Two, damaged his country's international reputation. His thirty-five years in power are rivalled in length only by Castro (see page 164) and Kim Il-sung (see page 116).

AUGUSTO PINOCHET
(1915–2006)

In a nutshell
Few of the modern brutal dictators have ever been brought to justice, but Augusto Pinochet, who tortured thousands of political opponents, spent the last few years of his life wriggling on the hook to avoid trial for corruption and murders when he died in December 2006.

Rise and rule
Pinochet was a career soldier whose apparent lack of political ambition turned to his advantage when Chilean president Salvador Allende appointed him commander in chief of the army in 1973.

The socialist government had made huge changes to Chile since coming to power in 1970, nationalising copper-mining companies and cultivating similarly-minded governments in Cuba, the USSR and China. This was too much for the US and its powerful business interests, and in 1973 the CIA helped to fund a bloody military coup. Allende either shot himself or was killed when the presidential palace was overrun, and Pinochet assumed power. He immediately suspended parliament, banned political and trade union activity and took sole power the following year.

Two decades of killing and torture followed as

Pinochet ruled Chile in a climate of fear. His secret police kidnapped thousands of opponents, many of whom were never found and are referred to as 'the disappeared'. His regime was tolerated by Western powers, which saw him as a bulwark against Communism.

Downfall

The economy took a downward turn in 1982, igniting civil unrest, and rebel guerrilla activity increased. In 1988, a constitutional plebiscite was held, and Pinochet expected to be given another eight years in office. When fifty-five per cent of voters put their mark against him, his power was diminished and he resigned in 1990. Visiting England for medical treatment in 1998, he was dramatically arrested for murder on a Spanish warrant. He pleaded illness and was allowed back to Chile, where he repeated this defence when indicted again. Some governments are still trying to bring him to trial. After a heart attack, Pinochet died in hospital in December 2006, aged 91.

What was he like?

Pinochet had the arrogance of a man with friends in high places. He showed utter disdain for the rights of any who opposed him, and sanctioned countless tortures and killings. He siphoned away millions of dollars into secret accounts, for which he was facing charges of forgery and tax fraud when he died.

Today's take

The Chilean economy was in crisis in 1973, having all but collapsed. It flourished for a period under Pinochet, and the bosses were well rewarded – while workers' pay rates fell. Some believe he saved Chile from Communism and created a free market platform for economic prosperity. Others see him as the man who ended many proud years of democracy. Stories of the barbarous punishments and executions committed on Pinochet's behalf have made his name synonymous with merciless contempt for human rights.

FERDINAND MARCOS
(1917–1989)

In a nutshell

Ferdinand Marcos was one of the most corrupt politicians in modern history, amassing a multi-billion dollar fortune at the expense of his country, the Philippines.

Rise and rule

Marcos employed his considerable skills as a lawyer to argue his way from his condemned cell to acquittal while on a charge of murdering one of his father's political rivals in 1939. He served without distinction in the Philippine Army during World War Two, but later claimed to have led the resistance movement, building a political career on this fiction. He switched his political allegiance to achieve nomination for the presidential elections, which he won in 1965.

He declared martial law in 1972 during a bout of social unrest that he had instigated. He proceeded to force his opponents into exile, to dissolve congress and to confiscate numerous businesses, which he handed over to his family, friends and close associates. Together with his wife Imelda, he pursued an extravagant lifestyle funded by corruption and looting of the treasury, appointing family members in key government posts. Nine years on, he ended martial law in return for a papal visit, but retained his dictatorial powers to arrest and detain without charge. Opposition leader Benigno Aquino Jnr. was assassinated on the tarmac of the airport when he returned to the country in 1983.

Downfall

Marcos's grasp of power was weakened by long absences for kidney treatment, during which there was a void at the centre of government. He called a snap election in 1986, to try to see off Aquino's wife, Corazon, but the result was disputed. Sensing rising popular resentment, he fled to Hawaii, where he died three years later.

Petty change

'I get so tired listening to one million dollars here, one million dollars there; it's so petty.'

Imelda Marcos,
after being questioned about where all the money went.

What was he like?

Marcos wanted to establish a family dynasty, and pursued a cult of personality (at one time his image was carved into a hillside, Mount Rushmore-style). Manipulative, corrupt and self-seeking, he projected himself internationally as a great leader and an enemy of Communism.

Today's take

During the twenty-one-year Marcos reign, there were episodes of economic growth, stimulated by farming subsidies, tourism and encouraging the unemployed to find work abroad. Marcos succeeded in taking apart a corrupt oligarchy, but then created one of his own, killing and torturing his people, looting their money and demolishing the legislative and judicial infrastructure.

Ferdinand Marcos is now regarded as a ruthless racketeer who exploited his own country to enrich his family and friends, leaving lasting damage to the political, social and economic framework of the Philippines.

NICOLAE CEAUSESCU
(1918–1989)

In a nutshell

Nicolae Ceausescu lived in palatial luxury while the starving Romanian people loaded up their crops for export. He turned his country into a nightmarish police state where, for twenty-four years, almost every aspect of life was ruled by his whims.

Rise and rule

An ardent, campaigning Communist, Ceausescu was repeatedly imprisoned for political activity in his youth. When the Romanian Workers' Party seized power in 1947, he became a minister and was appointed to the party central committee in 1952. In 1965, Ceausescu became leader of Romania, and earned some international respect and popularity by refusing to kowtow to the USSR's foreign policy.

Ironically, on the domestic scene he was establishing a state of which Stalin would have been proud: he set up a secret police that could arrest anyone thought to be a class enemy; he tore down ancient villages to put up apartment blocks; he attempted massive industrialisation funded by foreign debt; he set up work camps for prisoners and dissidents who were forced to endure primitive conditions; and he hounded the minority Hungarian populace.

Obsessed with building up the Romanian population, in 1966 Ceausescu banned contraception and abortion and set birth targets for women, establishing a punitive tax rate for those who stayed childless. Backstreet abortions soared, bringing enormous suffering to women and their unborn foetuses, and orphanages were filled with abandoned babies. Many women were reluctant to bring more children into the family as food was in short supply – Ceausescu was so desperate to pay off foreign debts he was exporting everything his country produced. State-controlled television showed him strolling around well-stocked shops, while the viewers reflected on the hours they spent queuing for necessities every day. Some of them were also aware that the foreign loans had largely been used to finance the building of various luxurious palaces in which Ceausescu and his wife disported themselves among collections of fur coats, shoes and tailor-made suits.

Downfall

Completely out of touch with the growing discontent of the Romanian people, Ceausescu held a public rally in Bucharest's main square. Live television coverage transmitted his bemused expression as the 80,000-strong crowd started to heckle him, before the broadcast was halted abruptly. In a chaotic end to his reign, he was driven aimlessly around the country, looking for an escape route, before he was recognised and handed over to the army. A military tribunal heard evidence of his mass murders and other crimes, and both Ceausescu and his wife were executed in the courtyard outside.

What was he like?
Ceausescu had a genuine passion for ideas, which then became twisted into warped self-regard. He awarded himself title after title (one of which was 'Genius of the Carpathians') while his uneducated wife, Elena (allegedly the architect of some of his crazy policies), tried to present herself as a scientist of international note. 'Deluded' doesn't come close to describing their fantasy world.

Today's take
Ceausescu virtually destroyed the Romanian economy and caused boundless suffering to his people. The country held its first free elections for fifty years within months of his death.

MOHAMMAD REZA PAHLAVI
(1919–1980)

In a nutshell

Considered by the Western powers as a more malleable leader than his father, Mohammad Reza Pahlavi, the Shah of Iran, eventually fell out with both the West and his people, leaving Iran to the rigours of fundamentalist Islamic rule.

Rise and rule

In 1941, the Allied powers, alarmed at the prospect of a neutral Iran coming under German control, deposed the shah – or king – and installed instead his twenty-one-year-old son. After being forced out of the country by a government that had, crucially and fatally, nationalised Iran's oil industry, the West backed him again, and he returned to rule with increasing autocracy.

He followed policies of modernisation and repression, giving women more rights on the one hand, but establishing and running the SAVAK secret police, who were infamous for their brutal persecution and torture of dissidents, on the other. He justified such repression by insisting he was fighting Communist influence, which appealed to his chief allies, Israel and the US. The Shah maintained good relations with the other Persian Gulf states, depicting himself as Iran's guardian, although there was frequent tension with neighbouring Iraq. However, the reforms of his White Revolution of 1963 outraged fundamentalist Islamic clerics – who became an increasing threat to his authority – while the West found his repressive methods less and less to its taste. In 1975, he turned Iran into a one-party state.

Downfall

In 1979, Muslim influence and Western lack of enthusiasm for his autocratic methods finally made the Shah's rule untenable, and he went into exile. He died the following year.

What was he like?

Mohammad Reza Pahlavi saw himself as part of an ancient royal dynasty, famously celebrating in 1975 the 2,500th anniversary of the Persian Empire with a three-day, multi-million-dollar party, catered for by 200 chefs jetted in from Paris. A manipulator rather than leader, he failed to gain the support of his people, who viewed him as corrupt and decadent.

Today's take

Iran prospered in the 1960s and 1970s because of its enormous oil deposits. However, the Shah became a hate figure to his own people and lost his value to the Western allies, who had twice put him into power.

MOHAMED SIAD BARRE
(1919–1995)

In a nutshell

Mohamed Siad Barre ruled Somalia as a military dictatorship for twenty-two years, vigorously pursuing a policy of tribal warfare and exploiting the aid offered – first by the Soviet Union then the US – to maintain his regime.

Rise and rule

Siad Barre rose from nothing: he was an orphaned shepherd with no formal education. He was heavily influenced by the Italian colonial police force, with whom he served for many years (Somalia gained independence from Italy in 1960), and was an advocate of Marxism.

By 1969, he was a general, and seized power in a military coup after the assassination of President Abdirashid Ali Shermarke ended Somalia's brief experience of democracy. He nationalised most of the economy and declared Somalia to be a socialist state, installing members of his own Marehan clan into key positions of power excluding others such as the Mijertyn and Issaq. Barre increased the size of the Somali army much to the consternation of neighbours such as Ethiopia and Kenya. Internally, he imposed the

Somali language on schools, probably in an attempt to unify the country, but it proved unsuitable for scientific and commercial development. He espoused a blend of Marxism and Islam and depicted himself in huge public portraits as a paternalistic leader. He even produced his own little blue and white book of sayings, echoing the practice of Mao Zedong in China (see page 90).

Somalia's key strategic location at the entrance to the Red Sea encouraged interest from the superpowers in the Cold War. The Soviet Union initially backed Barre's government, but they fell out in 1977 when he tried to invade part of neighbouring Ethiopia. The US stepped in with economic and military aid.

Opposition from excluded groups built up, and Barre's regime dealt brutally with separatist rebels, destroying whole settlements, killing 50,000 people and forcing possibly ten times that number to flee into Ethiopia. They returned to find their homes had been looted and mined by the army. Others who were imprisoned found that torture of political detainees was standard.

Downfall

Mass starvation and pressure from opposition clans eventually made his position untenable and Siad Barre fled into exile in Nigeria in 1991, leaving behind him a country that had descended into famine and anarchy. He died from a heart attack in 1995.

What was he like?

Barre attempted to set up a personality cult, calling himself 'Victorious Leader' and 'Father of Wisdom'. He showed great loyalty to his own tribe at the expense of other Somali groups, and is regarded as a ruthless tyrant.

Today's take

Barre was not alone in being unable or unwilling to try to unite Somalia. His 'Ugly Revolution' ended democracy in the country, and Somalia has had no effective national government since his fall.

GEORGE PAPADOPOULOS
(1919–1999)

In a nutshell

For six years from 1967, a military government ruled Greece. The military junta was known as the Regime of the Generals, and its de facto head was George Papadopoulos, a man who saw Communist threats everywhere, and used them as an excuse for retaining total control of the country.

Rise and rule

During World War Two, Papadopoulos allegedly worked for the Nazi occupation forces, helping to collect local taxes and combating the Communist resistance forces. He built his own power base in the army and in 1967 mounted a successful coup, backed by fellow generals alarmed at the prospect of leftist success in the impending elections.

The generals claimed they were acting to prevent a Communist takeover, but there was no such threat (such was Papadopoulos' obsession with Communism that he once accused ex-US President Richard Nixon and most of the American Congress of having Communist sympathies). King Constantine made one hapless attempt at a counter coup but was forced into exile.

    With the Cold War at its height, Papadopoulos enjoyed the support of the US and other Western powers. He imposed martial law, blocked free speech and arrested and tortured many people with supposed left-wing sympathies, while trying to impose new standards in Greek life by banning mini skirts and long hair. Unable to get his wife to agree to a divorce, he arranged a temporary change in the law to allow him to divorce her and then marry his mistress.

Downfall

In June 1973, he appointed himself president, making Greece a republic. That November, there was a student uprising at the University of Athens. Papadopoulos used the army to quell the unrest, killing twenty students in the process, but fellow generals were afraid he might be tempted into democratic reforms to sustain his own position, so they ousted him. Greece remained under military rule for a further nine months, until democracy was restored in 1974. Papadopoulos was later convicted of treason, but escaped the death sentence. When the government suggested they would free him on humanitarian grounds in December 1990 there was a public outcry and he remained incarcerated until he died in 1999.

What was he like?
Papadopoulos had two key characteristics that coloured everything he did: he was obsessively anti-Communist, and he was a patriot. He had few talents and no political vision, but he was highly ambitious, and in the conditions of the time, that was enough.

Today's take
Papadopoulos is remembered as an autocratic leader who, with his violent contempt for human rights, brought international disgrace upon Greece.

JEAN-BÉDEL BOKASSA
(1921–1996)

In a nutshell

Bokassa is notorious for the depths of his extravagance, and for the accusation that, in addition to terrorising and robbing his people, he also ate them.

Rise and rule

Bokassa took the standard route to dictatorship of the Central African Republic, rising to head the army before ousting President Dacko in 1966. He appointed himself to key government posts and was personally involved in the beating and killing of opponents.

In 1977, he proclaimed himself emperor at a lavish two-day ceremony, in which a diamond-studded crown was placed on his head as he sat on a two-tonne solid gold throne. The international community stayed away, but France, keen to exploit the Central African Republic's uranium resources for its nuclear programme, remained a key ally and contributor of 'humanitarian aid', which was redirected to Bokassa's account. Bokassa's coronation cost a whopping US$20 million, which was a quarter of the Central African Republic's revenue.

He decreed that all schoolchildren should wear the overpriced uniforms produced at his own factory, and in 1979 supervised the massacre of a hundred of them who protested about it. On this occasion, as on others, he is said to have eaten the bodies of his victims.

Downfall

The madness could not last, and later that year Bokassa was ousted in a French-led coup that brought President Dacko back to power. Bokassa went into luxurious exile at a château near Paris. In a bizarre postscript, he returned to the Republic in 1986 to face charges of treason, murder, embezzlement and cannibalism, and was convicted of all except the last. After six years in solitary confinement he was freed. He died from a heart attack in 1996.

What was he like?

Fixated by Napoleon, Bokassa had a monumental ego that was matched only by his relish for violence. He successfully cultivated the friendship of French President Valéry Giscard d'Estaing, taking him on hunting trips and giving him presents of diamonds.

And for dessert?

After he fled, the freezer in Bokassa's old palace was found to contain the body of a schoolteacher hanging on a hook above mounds of other human flesh waiting to be cooked.

Today's take

Bokassa's reign shows how a crucial foreign backer can keep even the most decadent regime in power. He bankrupted his country with his extravagance and embezzlement.

HAJI MOHAMED SUHARTO
(1921–)

In a nutshell
Suharto ran a repressive regime with scant regard for human rights in Indonesia and, after invading it, East Timor. He also earned a reputation as one of the most corrupt leaders of modern times, feathering his own nest so abundantly that he has been ranked the sixth-richest person in the world.

Rise and rule
Suharto's predecessor was Achmed Sukarno, who alienated the West by siding with the Soviet Union during the Cold War. The US in particular welcomed it when the obscure commander of the Jakarta garrison, General Suharto, started murdering Communists, forced the president into retirement and took over the presidency in 1966. By the time he reached power, it is estimated that half a million Indonesians with left-wing sympathies had been killed by the army, police and vigilantes.

Suharto was elected president in 1968, and repeated the exercise every five years until 1988. Each election was fixed and, in effect, uncontested. His strongman tactics brought stability after years of social upheaval. Suharto sought Western investment, especially in

Indonesia's mining and construction interests, and averted a crisis in food production.

Under his so-called New Order government, foreign businesses were encouraged to invest in Indonesia through intermediaries appointed by the president: they were invariably members either of his family, the military or his Golkar party. Bribery, racketeering and embezzlement became routine. Suharto and his family were major players, building an enormous fortune out of banking, wheat production, and the car and cigarette industries. They also lifted most of the US$43 billion aid supplied by the International Monetary Fund. Suharto became the sixth richest person in the world with an estimated personal fortune of US$16 billion, more than half of it deposited in an Austrian bank.

In 1975, Suharto invaded neighbouring East Timor in a bid to block Communist subversion. At least 100,000 people were killed by the Indonesian police or army, many of them innocent civilians, and Suharto's family took over about forty per cent of the conquered land.

Downfall

The end of the Cold War reduced Suharto's importance to the West, and the 1991 Dili Massacre of unarmed Timorese attending a funeral placed greater international scrutiny on his record of human rights abuses. With his international reputation in decline, Suharto's domestic standing also plummeted after a major financial crisis in 1997 forced him to implement austerity measures that pushed prices up dramatically. Although he won the 1998 election, his own party and the military had lost faith in him, and he stood down that May.

What's he like?
Suharto was heavily influenced by the nationalist and militarist ideology inculcated in the Japanese-sponsored military, with whom he trained. He projected himself as the unbending father of the nation. In fact, his major characteristic seems to have been greed.

Today's take
Under Suharto, Indonesia was strong and relatively stable, and its economy boomed. The number of Indonesians living in absolute poverty fell from sixty per cent to fourteen per cent between 1970 and 1990. He benefited more than anybody else from this, and the price his people paid was fear of mass killings, their non-existent human rights and endemic corruption in business. When the economy collapsed, Suharto's money was safely banked out of the country.

ROBERT MUGABE *(1924–)*

In a nutshell

Although he has been voted into power several times, Mugabe is regarded as a dictator because these elections have been increasingly rigged and because of his violent, autocratic, anti-democratic method of government.

Rise and rule

Mugabe studied education and worked training teachers in Ghana. However, he had become a committed Marxist and he returned to Zimbabwe (then known as Rhodesia) in 1960 to join the opposition ZAPU (Zimbabwe African People's Union) and then the ZANU (Zimbabwe African National Union) movements. Under Rhodesia's laws of summary imprisonment, this led to him spending ten years in jail from 1964, during which time he studied law. After this he retreated to Mozambique from where he led an armed guerilla struggle against Ian Smith's white government, and was regarded internationally as a freedom fighter.

After Britain and the US rejected the 1979 elections because groups such as Mugabe's were not represented, new elections were held the following year and Mugabe scraped home to lead an uneasy coalition. He consolidated his position by political manoeuvring and using the military to crush resistance brutally, assuming the role of president in 1987. He was re-elected in 1990, 1996 and 2002. In many of these elections, he used a system of patronage of village elders to boost the vote and has closed polling stations in regions that do not support him. Various other irregularities, which amount to him rigging the vote, have been reported.

In addition, his supporters have been rewarded with land and food at a time of enormous economic difficulty, mostly of Mugabe's own making. Since 1999, he has seized numerous rich, fertile white-owned farms and handed them to 'war veterans', most of whom are too young to have fought for him. In 2005, he bulldozed tens of thousands of urban homes, leaving their occupiers without shelter. City dwellers have traditionally opposed Mugabe.

Guns and votes

'Our votes must go together with our guns.
After all, any vote we shall have shall have been the
product of the gun. The gun which produces
the vote should remain its security officer – its guarantor.
The people's votes and the people's guns
are always inseparable twins.'

Robert Mugabe speaking in 1976.

Downfall

Mugabe remains in power, although outside Africa he is a pariah.

What's he like?

Mugabe cuts an arrogant figure, but he is also a wily politician who has frequently out-manoeuvred his opponents – and who uses violence or arrest when they still pose a threat. He is vigorously homophobic, which feeds his lack of interest in combating HIV/AIDS and has led to an epidemic of the disease in Zimbabwe.

Public respect for him fell when he announced he had married his former private secretary (with whom he had sired two children) in an African ceremony, even though he was already married and had professed to be Catholic.

Today's take

Zimbabwe was once self-sufficient, but Mugabe has turned southern Africa's breadbasket into a basket-case economy where the people starve amid mounting unemployment. Regarded as a ruthless dictator by many, he is still seen as a hero by some Africans because of his anti-colonial stance.

IDI AMIN (c. 1925–2003)

In a nutshell

Sometimes depicted as an eccentric buffoon, Idi Amin was a murderously violent dictator who did enormous damage to Uganda's people, economy and reputation.

Rise and rule

Born into poverty, Amin was poorly educated but proved a loyal soldier serving in the British forces until independence in 1962. He was one of the first two Ugandans to become an officer in 1961, and rose to the rank of chief of staff in 1966. From this position of control, he was able to lead a bloody coup in January 1971 while the current president, Milton Oboto, was out of the country. Anyone who angered him risked torture, death and dismemberment, and Amin ruled by a series of bizarre decrees including the banning of hippies and mini skirts.

In 1972, he exiled 50,000 people of Asian descent, who ran many of Uganda's businesses and formed its

Not so bright

When he was a soldier Amin was 'virtually bone from the neck up and needs things explained in words of one letter'

according to an (anonymous) British diplomat.

middle class, plunging the economy into chaos and prompting the withdrawal of much foreign aid.
He also sanctioned the torture and killing of up to half a million Ugandans from other tribes. Decapitated and otherwise mutilated bodies were displayed regularly, and human remains were fed to the crocodiles of the River Nile.

Amin awarded himself numerous military medals and titles, including, bizarrely, calling himself King of Scotland. Ever eager to pronounce on the world stage, he sounded off about Northern Ireland and Vietnam, and betrayed his past allies the Israelis by backing the Palestinian cause.

This was his motive for helping hijackers of a French jet carrying many Jewish passengers, which was forced to land at Entebbe airport in Uganda in June 1976. The Israelis rescued the hostages and crew in a remarkable long-range raid, killing twenty Ugandan soldiers in the process. As a result, the Ugandan Army apparently killed an English woman, Dora Bloch – who had been taken from the plane to hospital – and dumped her body in a forest. Britain broke off diplomatic relations a month later.

Not so tasty
'I want to eat your heart, I want to eat your children.'

Amin to advisor,
just before dinner.

Downfall

Amin provoked his neighbour Tanzania into invading Uganda in January 1979, and he fled the country soon after. He spent ten years in Libya before moving to Saudi Arabia, where he died in 2003.

What was he like?

Poorly educated, but tall and athletic, Amin was Ugandan heavyweight boxing champion and treated all his opponents like a punchbag. The cruel punishments and murders carried out and encouraged by him bordered on the psychotic.

Today's take

Amin did untold damage to his own country, exiling or murdering hundreds of thousands of them and reversing the growth of a vibrant economy. It seems incredible that his rule was tolerated for so long – by his own people, and by the international community.

FIDEL CASTRO *(1926–)*

In a nutshell
Fidel Castro is one of the most successful modern dictators, having been in power since 1959. He gets an easier ride in Western political circles than other brutal rulers because left-wing elements are reluctant to criticise a Communist dictator.

Rise and rule
Born into a wealthy farming family, Castro shone as a student and athlete at school. He graduated in law in 1950 and was already heavily influenced by Marxism-Leninism and had

Why I am in charge
'The revolution is a dictatorship of the exploited against the exploiters.'

Fidel Castro

developed a particular antipathy to American corporate culture. Three years later, he took up arms against Cuban leader Fulgencio Batista, hoping to spark a popular revolt. He failed, and after two years in jail was released into exile in Mexico. In 1959, he tried again, backed by his guerilla force known as the 26th of July Movement, named after the date of his 1953 attack.

This time his revolutionary ideas caught the public's imagination, and he ousted Batista. Soon he nationalised US-owned properties and businesses, mainly fruit-growing concerns. He further alarmed his near neighbour by cosying up to the Soviet Union, which propped up his government.

In Castro's regime, public criticism is forbidden. Journalists must follow the government line, and any in the media who dare to attack Castro face lengthy sentences in jails notorious for beatings and punishment. Castro is renowned for the interminable length of his public speeches in which he rages against the evils of capitalism. He has survived hundreds of assassination plots – many funded by the CIA – and has become a major bogeyman for his powerful neighbour.

Penny for your thoughts

'Castro couldn't even go to the bathroom unless the Soviet Union put the nickel in the toilet.'

US president Richard Nixon, clearly not a fan.

Downfall

Castro remains in power, but failing health and the disappearance of support from the collapsed Soviet Union suggest that his days could be numbered.

What's he like?

Castro was heavily influenced by Mussolini's rhetorical and theatrical style and is a master of the public gesture. Unusually for a dictator, he keeps his family out of the spotlight, although his brother Raul serves as first deputy prime minister. Despite claiming to support family values, Castro is known for his love of women and has fathered many children out of wedlock.

Today's take

Castro's main achievement has been to stay in power despite the hostility felt towards him by his neighbour, the most powerful nation in the world, which famously attempted an invasion at the Bay of Pigs in 1961. Cuba was internationally isolated, but has managed to retain China as a powerful ally and is becoming a popular tourist destination. It has good welfare, health and education systems, but many restrictions on business and freedom of expression. Much of its middle class has fled to American exile.

POL POT *(1928–1998)*

In a nutshell
Pol Pot took his own country back to the middle ages in a bid to create an agrarian utopia. In the process, up to two million of his people either starved to death or were killed for questioning his dogma.

Rise and rule
Born to a well-off rice farmer, the young Pol Pot did not have to tend the fields but was sent away to study Buddhism (the main religion of his country) before going to college and eventually completing a course in radio technology in Paris. He became an active Communist, neglecting his studies and failing his exams before returning to Cambodia to campaign against the government.

Over years of struggle, he developed an admiration for the simple life of the rural communities amongst which he lived, and for the methods of mind control used by Mao Zedong during China's Cultural Revolution (see page 90). Aided by resentment at American bombing of Cambodia as part of its war in Vietnam, Pol Pot's Chinese-backed Khmer Rouge army grew to 100,000-strong and swept into power, taking the capital Phnom Penh in 1975. The country was renamed Democratic Kampuchea.

He then began an extraordinary attempt to destroy urban life by forcing the entire population to work on communal rural farms. Religion, local customs and languages and meaningful education were all banned, and family life was consigned to the past: the government took the place of parents, and Pol Pot was known as Brother Number One. Three classes were created: the uneducated peasantry, who had full rights and could claim proper rations; a second category of candidates who had to prove their worth to join the ranks of the first group; and the depositees. This final group comprised the educated urban dwellers. They had no rights and were fed starvation rations of two bowls of rice soup a day.

Those who dared question the rules by which they had to live were 're-educated' at detention camps, where they were tortured to force them to admit to bourgeois sins such as meeting missionaries or engaging in free-market activity. They were the lucky ones: estimates of how many people died from starvation or execution vary between one and two million. At execution sites, known as the 'killing fields', victims were despatched with sharpened bamboo sticks, iron bars or hoes, in an effort to save bullets. Sometimes, they were buried alive. Eight thousand skulls were found at one mass grave alone.

Downfall

Conditions were so poor that even the Khmer Rouge army was starving. They were no match for the

Vietnamese forces who, after years of border disputes, invaded in January 1979. Pol Pot fled to the hill country from where he continued the fight, eventually resigning from the Khmer Rouge in 1985. Two years later his former colleagues charged him with treason and he was put under house arrest. He died, probably from a heart attack, in 1998.

No problem

'I did not join the resistance movement to kill people, to kill the nation. Look at me now. Am I a savage person? My conscience is clear.'

Pol Pot
towards the end of his life.

What was he like?

Perhaps deliberately, Pol Pot was a largely anonymous figure for years: few knew who he was when he took power, and his own brother was amazed when he learned his sibling was leader of the Khmer Rouge. His mediocre academic record may help to explain his hatred of intellectuals, but his relish of the punishments meted out to them borders on the psychotic, and the killing of any perceived plotter or rival suggests total paranoia.

Today's take
In his determination to create a rural paradise, Pol Pot was responsible for the deaths of a quarter of his people and in terms of development, led his country backwards.

MOBUTU SESE SEKO
(1930–1997)

In a nutshell
Mobutu meets most of the criteria for the successful modern dictator: he used violence to gain power, and money to retain it, supported all the while by major powers who preferred his brand of politics to what might replace it in Zaire.

Rise and rule
From a background as a soldier then a journalist, Mobutu was already a minister in the newly independent Congo when he supported a coup in 1960. Five years on, backed by Belgium and the CIA, he seized power. Political foes, such as the previous Prime Minister Evariste Kimba, were publicly hanged as a warning to others.

In 1970, he consolidated power by declaring his Popular Movement of the Revolution (MPR) as the country's only political party and was elected unopposed as president. From his secure position he changed tack, shunning Western powers and, in his unique way, encouraging African culture – for example, priests faced death if they baptised someone with a European name rather than an African one. Public demonstrations were banned, as were many religions.

He seized foreign assets and gave them to his relatives and close associates, using the money gained to bribe opponents rather than butcher them, therefore tying them to his regime. He was the greatest beneficiary of the giant rake-off of assets and aid, garnering a fortune estimated at US$4–$5 billion.

When the economy inevitably collapsed he sought international aid, receiving $12 billion from powers frightened at the prospect of Communism spreading from neighbouring Angola. In 1978, France, Belgium and the US backed him against a domestic revolt.

Downfall

With the end of the Cold War, Mobutu lost Western support and the deteriorating economy prompted further unrest. An uncomfortable power-sharing arrangement was forged in 1991, but his army bolstered his continued dominance until he was finally expelled in 1997. He died shortly afterwards in Morocco.

What was he like?

Mobutu operated a personality cult, and the image of him with his leather walking cane and leopard-skin cap dominated the media. His 1972 adoption of the name Mobutu Sese Seko Nkuku Ngbendu Wa Za Banga ('The all-powerful warrior who, because of his

endurance and inflexible will to win, will go from
conquest to conquest, leaving fire in his wake'),
encapsulates his ego.

Today's take
Mobutu united the 200 tribes of his young country
and prompted pride in a new national identity,
but he also robbed his own land and left it
impoverished and unstable. Zaire is now known
as the Democratic Republic of Congo.

SADDAM HUSSEIN *(1937–)*

In a nutshell

Saddam Hussein is an Arab Josef Stalin: a leader who inspires terror, distrusts colleagues, has a liking for violence and who values his own reputation more than that of his country.

Rise and rule

Born in a Sunni Muslim village just outside Tikrit in 1937, Saddam was poorly educated, partly because his stepfather put him to work stealing sheep rather than sending him to school. Saddam became heavily involved in the Ba'ath Party, and, after the monarchy was overthrown in 1959, he was involved in a plot to kill prime minister Abdul-Karim Qassim. He fled to Egypt, returning when the Ba'ath Party briefly regained power. He became its assistant general secretary in 1966 and, when it seized control in yet another coup two years later, he was at the centre of government under Ahmad Hassan al-Bakr, heading up the secret police and responsible for torturing political suspects.

In 1979, he forced the ailing al-Bakr to resign and became president. In a chilling episode, recorded on video, he called a meeting of Ba'ath leaders and read out a list of sixty-eight rivals. Each was led out of the room while he praised the loyalty of the terrified audience still in their seats. Twenty-two of the group were later shot.

He launched an invasion of neighbouring Iran in 1980, but was surprised by its refusal to capitulate. The war eventually ended in stalemate eight years later, after the deaths of hundreds of thousands of troops on both sides. Ronald Reagan's US government supported him, seeing him as a safeguard against an anti-Western fundamentalist Muslim state. The US ignored Hussein's use of chemical weapons against independence-seeking Kurdish rebels in northern Iraq.

In August 1990, he invaded the small kingdom of Kuwait in order to take over its lucrative oil fields. This alarmed Western powers, already concerned by indications that Saddam was trying to develop weapons of mass destruction. After fruitless months of diplomatic manoeuvring, the Iraqi army was driven back in early 1991. Crucially, the US-led forces did not turf out Saddam, and he continued to persecute the factions that opposed him. He drained the waters in Shia territory in the south, forcing the Marsh Arabs off their homelands. Opponents were massacred in trenches they had been made to dig, before soil was bulldozed over their bodies.

Downfall

International sanctions crippled the Iraqi economy. In March 2003, US and UK forces invaded, saying Saddam was a supporter of international terrorism and possessed weapons of mass destruction. They easily defeated a disorganised and poorly equipped army, and Saddam went into hiding. He was captured eight months later and put on trial for mass killings. In November 2006 he was found guilty of crimes against humanity and sentenced to death.

What's he like?

Saddam took the concept of a personality cult to new heights, putting up posters and statues around the country and depicting himself as the father of the nation. He trusted only some of his close family members and a few others, and dealt quickly and ruthlessly with perceived threats – he once asked a minister to leave a cabinet meeting, shot him dead and calmly returned to the gathering.

Mother of all quotes

'The great duel, the mother of all battles, has begun. The dawn of victory nears as this great showdown begins.'

Saddam Hussein
soon after the beginning of the American Desert Storm attack, January 1991.

Today's take

Saddam succeeded in holding Iraq together by terrorising its people. Some Arabs admire his resilience against Western influence and his consistent animosity to Israel. He bankrupted Iraq with ill-judged wars when he could have built up its economy with its plentiful oil resources.

KIM JONG-IL *(1941–)*

In a nutshell

In a unique instance of a dictatorial dynasty continuing, Kim Jong-il took his father's place as the leader of North Korea. He has continued the policies of isolationism and heavy military expenditure which, to outsiders, bring only harm to his country.

Rise and rule

As is the way in North Korea, facts are changed to give the right impression. So Kim's unremarkable 1941 birth in Soviet Siberia is officially presented as taking place the next year (symbolically his father's thirtieth), in a log cabin on Korea's highest mountain, heralded by a double rainbow and a bright new star.

Cheers!

Kim has a luxury home in each of North Korea's eight provinces. There he can choose what to watch from his collection of 20,000 films, while knocking back Hennessy VSOP Cognac – he allegedly spends more than $650,000 a year on the drink.

Most dictators fight their way to the top. Kim merely stepped into his father's built-up shoes (both men tried to conceal their lack of height). He was given a series of jobs in the ruling Korean Workers' Party and the government and was publicly referred to as the Dear Leader – a clear sign that he would succeed to power – while his only possible rival, the unrelated Prime Minister Kim Il, lost his position in 1976. Crucially, Kim Jong-il became head of the North Korean army in 1991, despite his lack of military experience. Already de facto national leader, he took over completely when his father died in 1994.

Stay away from me

In 2003, Kim ordered the removal from their homes of all triplets, who were to be placed in orphanages. Ostensibly a policy to help the poor, it is more likely that Kim was feeling threatened by the popular Korean superstition that triplets rise to positions of power, and was trying to control their lives so that they could not replace him.

Since then he has pursued policies of self-reliance, which cause enormous hardship to his people, although some market reforms have been introduced. He is also believed to have given North Korea nuclear weapons capability. He has built his own personality cult, and is hailed in the state-controlled media as the 'peerless leader'.

Downfall
He remains in power.

What's he like?
Kim Jong-il has a reputation as a vain playboy. He is rarely seen in public and hardly ever travels abroad, possibly for fear of what could happen in his absence – although he also has a phobia of flying. His only recorded public utterance was at a military parade in 1992, when he said, 'Glory to the heroic soldiers of the people's army.'

> **Today's take**
> Kim follows in his father's footsteps, secure in power but achieving little internationally. US president George W. Bush included North Korea in his 'Axis of Evil' powers alongside Iran and Iraq, mainly because of Kim's nuclear aspirations.

SAPARMURAT NIYAZOV
(1940–)

In a nutshell
Niyazov treats Turkmenistan – once part of the Soviet Union – as his personal fiefdom, which he rules with eccentric zeal.

Rise and rule
Niyazov's father died during World War Two and the rest of his family were killed in a 1948 earthquake, so he was raised in a Soviet orphanage before living with a distant relative.

He was a key figure in the Communist Party when his country was part of the Soviet Union and became its first president after it achieved independence in 1991. He began championing traditional Turkmen culture, rejecting Russian and Western influences such as opera, ballet and universities. Instead, he brought in a new Turkmen alphabet and renamed the days and months after

> **Where the sun shines**
> *A huge golden statue of Niyazov in a billowing golden cloak dominates the Turkmenistan capital, Ashgabat. It turns through 360 degrees every day so that his face always catches the sun.*

national heroes and symbols. The 'official' culture is described in his own book *Ruhnama*, a historical and spiritual tome, which is required reading for the five million-strong population and virtually the only book available in the country.

Trade and legal disputes limit the use that can be made of Turkmenistan's considerable oil and gas reserves, and what revenue there is is frittered on grand projects rather than building a solid infrastructure.

Toothache

In 2004, there was a rush of people visiting the dentist to have their gold teeth removed after Niyazov complained too many people had gold crowns to conceal their rotted teeth.

He said 'I watched young dogs when I was young. They were given bones to gnaw. Those of you whose teeth have fallen out did not gnaw on bones.'

Niyazov's influence is everywhere: he decrees what schoolchildren should wear, disapproves of men having beards and long hair, and banned smoking after he quit for health reasons in 1997. He was proclaimed president for life in 1999. He is referred to as Turkmenbashi, or 'father of the Turkmen', and criticism of him is likely to lead to jail or exile. The media, Internet and email traffic are all controlled and monitored.

Downfall

Niyazov is still in power, despite an assassination attempt in 2002 and signs of unrest in 2004. He has suggested new elections may be held in 2009.

What's he like?

Niyazov has tried to re-brand his country in his own image. His portrait and statues are everywhere, while watches bearing his picture have been given to children, students and officers. He renamed a town after himself and even tried to change the traditional word for bread to that of his mother's name. He also banned lip-synching when performing songs.

Today's take

Niyazov's eccentricity is no joke to those who suffer under his rule. He has virtually cut off Turkmenistan from the rest of the world, running it as a one-party, almost a one-man, state.

MUAMMAR AL-GADDAFI
(1942–)

In a nutshell

Gaddafi is one of the most successful dictators in history: he has held power since 1969, and if anything has strengthened his grip on office since then to become the Arab world's longest serving leader.

Rise and rule

Born in a Bedouin desert tent, Gaddafi was a political activist from his teenage years, campaigning against imperialism and Libya's pro-Western monarchy. He read history and political science at university, where he abandoned his Marxist principles in favour of Islam. He joined the army after graduating in 1965, and four years later, while King Idris was abroad, pre-empted a coup by senior officers when he stormed the royal palace and key government offices to seize power for himself.

Femme fatales

Wherever he goes, Gaddafi is protected by at least one of his group of about forty female bodyguards. They are specially trained in firearms and martial arts skills, and it is said he insists they remain virgins during their employ – although there are rumours that he is himself friendly with them beyond the call of duty.

He booted out the American and British from their military bases, and expelled most of Libya's native community of Jews and Italians as part of an anti-Western, pro-Arab policy. This stance was reflected in the support he gave to revolutionary and terrorist groups such as the IRA, the PLO, Black September and the Nation of Islam. He was able to finance this because in 1973 he nationalised Libya's considerable gas and oil resources.

Opposing views

'In the Middle East, the opposition is quite different than the opposition in advanced countries. In our countries, the opposition takes the form of explosions, assassinations, killings.'

Gaddafi knows his public.

Gaddafi imposed his own brand of Islamic socialism, banned alcohol and gambling and introduced a system of government known as *Jamahiriya*, in which power is supposedly held by people's committees. In reality, Gaddafi runs the show, using his hit squads to kill off opponents at home and abroad and imposing strict controls on the media.

Internationally, Gaddafi has tempered his Arab nationalism in a bid for more solidarity with other African states. He also accepted Libyan responsibility for the bombing of Pan Am Flight 103, which exploded over Scotland in 1988, possibly as a (successful) ploy to end the damaging UN sanctions against his country.

Downfall
He remains in power.

What's he like?
Gaddafi is a charismatic figure who has established a cult of personality in Libya, where he is referred to as 'Brotherly Leader and Guide of the Revolution'. Unusually for a military dictator, he has avoided adopting a higher rank than colonel.

Today's take
Despite several assassination attempts and continued friction with the US (which bombed Tripoli in 1986), Gaddafi has an iron grip on power and has steered Libya skilfully on a course in which the hated Westerners are allowed to help run the oil industry so essential to the economy without having much influence on the state.

Picture Credits